The Penguin Practical
The TOEFL® Test

DICTIONARY

Daniel de Souza

PENGUIN BOOKS

PENGUIN BOOKS

Published by the Penguin Group
Penguin Books Ltd, 27 Wrights Lane, London W8 5TZ, England
Penguin Books USA Inc., 375 Hudson Street, New York, New York 10014, USA
Penguin Books Australia Ltd, Ringwood, Victoria, Australia
Penguin Books Canada Ltd, 10 Alcorn Avenue, Toronto, Ontario, Canada M4V 3B2
Penguin Books (NZ) Ltd, 182-190 Wairau Road, Auckland 10, New Zealand

Penguin Books Ltd, Registered Offices: Harmondsworth, Middlesex, England

Published by Penguin Books 1997
10 9 8 7 6 5 4 3 2 1

Text copyright © Daniel de Souza 1997
All rights reserved

The moral right of the author has been asserted

Printed in England by Clays Ltd, St Ives plc
Designed in QuarkXpress on an Apple Macintosh
Set in Gill Sans and Bembo

Except in the United States of America, this book is sold subject to the condition that it shall not, by way of trade or otherwise, be lent, resold, hired out, or otherwise circulated without the publisher's prior consent in any form of binding or cover other than that in which it is published and without a similar condition including this condition being imposed on the subsequent purchaser

TOEFL is a registered trademark of Educational Testing Service
This publication has neither been reviewed nor endorsed by the ETS

Contents

Introduction	5
Alphabetical Listing	7
Structure and Vocabulary Checks	83
Answers	93

Introduction

The purpose of this specialized dictionary is to help students preparing for the TOEFL. At first sight, the vocabulary used in the exam would appear to be the most daunting aspect of the TOEFL. Although it is sometimes possible to guess approximate meanings, in many cases a knowledge of exact definitions and adjoining prepositions is crucial. The sheer number of words and alternative meanings listed by standard dictionaries make them unsuitable sources of reference as they tend to be more confusing than helpful. The prime difficulty in trying to prepare for the TOEFL is to discover which words are likely to crop up in the tests and how to memorize them. The aim of the *TOEFL Dictionary* is to ease this difficulty. Essentially it is a pre-exam 'crammer' catering only for the needs of those intending to take the TOEFL exam. To this end, this new dictionary varies in a number of significant ways from a conventional dictionary.

1   The words have been carefully researched and compiled from past TOEFL papers, other exams and related texts published by the US Education Testing Service (ETS), the creators of TOEFL.

2   In cases where words have more than one meaning, only a single definition has been given to illustrate the usage that appears frequently in the TOEFL.

3   The actual word-list has been reduced to the minimum and presented in a deliberately over-simplified manner so that the dictionary can be read and memorized rather than consulted.

4   For the same reason, a similar approach has been taken regarding derived words. Only unusual or easily con-

Introduction

fused forms have been listed; for example: most adverbs that are merely adjectives with the suffix *–ly* have been excluded. This economical approach has also been applied to the listing of adjoining prepositions and negative forms. Only those that appear frequently in the exam or are confusing have been included.

5. Very few technical words have been listed. Although many words relating to specialized fields are used in the exam, they are rarely tested with questions and a knowledge of their precise meanings is not normally necessary to understand the essential themes of the comprehension passages or to answer the structure questions.

Hints on Using the TOEFL Dictionary

Reading through the dictionary, students will find many words that are already familiar. These should be marked so that they can be immediately excluded from revision programs. Particular attention should be paid to adjoining prepositions and negative forms which are frequently tested in Section Two of TOEFL. Once the dictionary has been thoroughly studied, students should test themselves using the structure and vocabulary exercises at the end of the book.

Key

adv = adverb
adj = adjective
v = verb
n = noun
prep = preposition
pn = person noun
neg = negative

A

abate   *v* (to lessen; to subside) *He took an aspirin and waited for his headache to **abate**.*

abet   *v* (to encourage) *It is against the law to aid and **abet** a criminal.*

abhor   *v* (to hate; to detest) *He **abhorred** her rude manner.* ➤ *n* **abhorrence** (*prep* **of**); *adj* **abhorrent**

abject   *adj* (miserable; wretched) *Until he found work they lived in **abject** poverty.* ➤ *n* **abjection**; *adv* **abjectly**

abnormal   *adj* (not normal) *It was **abnormal** for the streets to be so quiet on a Saturday night.* ➤ *n* **abnormality**

abode   *n* (home) *He was once a millionaire but now his **abode** is a cardboard box.*

abolish   *v* (to bring to an end) *The battle to **abolish** slavery was hard fought.* ➤ *n* **abolition** (*prep* **of**); *pn* **abolitionist**

abrade   *v* (to wear away by rubbing) *The rough edge of the rock **abraded** the rope.* ➤ *n* **abrasion** (*prep* **of**); *adj* **abrasive**

abruptly   *adv* (suddenly; unexpectedly) *The train halted so **abruptly** that a passenger was hurt.* ➤ *n* **abruptness**; *adj* **abrupt**

absence   *n* (to be not present) *His **absence** was due to illness.* ➤ *adj* **absent** (*prep* **from**)

absorbed   *adj* (interested; engrossed) *Bill did not hear the telephone because he was completely **absorbed** in his reading.*

abstract   *v* (*prep* **from**) (to take from) *His words had been **abstracted** from a longer speech.* ➤ *n* **abstraction**; *adj* **abstract** (unreal)

abundant   *adj* (plentiful) *The crop was so **abundant** that the farmers had to store half of it.* ➤ *n* **abundance** (*prep* **of**)

abyss   *n* (bottomless hole) *He felt as if he'd fallen into an **abyss** of despair.*

accede   *v* (*prep* **to**) (to agree to a suggestion) *Finally, he **acceded** to the demand.* ➤ *n* **accession**

accelerate	*v* (to increase speed) *The powerful car quickly **accelerated** to its fastest speed.* ➤ *n* **acceleration**
access	*n* (**prep to**) (means of entering into or obtaining) *The gate was the only **access** to the building.* ➤ *v* **access**; *adj* **access**
accessory	*n* (something added; an extra) *The new Cadillac has many optional **accessories**.*
acclaim	*v* (to greet with praise) *The new drug has been **acclaimed** by many doctors.* ➤ *n* **acclaim**
accommodate	*v* (to make changes that allow for new requirements) *He was reluctant to **accommodate** her wishes but there was no alternative.* ➤ *n* **accommodation**
accomplice	*n* (one who aids a criminal) *The police are still looking for the robbers' **accomplice**.*
accomplish	*v* (to finish; to complete) *The student failed to **accomplish** the task he'd been set.* ➤ *n* **accomplishment**
accord	*n* (**prep with**) (to be in agreement) *Both sides are in **accord**, so a settlement may come soon.*
accost	*v* (to approach someone and to speak challengingly) *On leaving the office, Mary was **accosted** by a stranger asking for money.*
account	*v* (**prep for**) (to explain or relate) *Can you **account** for the fact you're late?* ➤ *n* **accountability**; *adj* **accountable**
accumulate	*v* (to pile up; to collect over time) *Look at all the fallen leaves that have **accumulated** in the garden.* ➤ *n* **accumulation** (**prep of**); *adj* **accumulative**
accurate	*adj* (correct) *Journalists have a reponsibility to write **accurate** reports.* ➤ *n* **accuracy**; *neg* **inaccurate**
accustom	*v* (**prep to**) (to get used to) *It took years for John to become **accustomed** to the weather.*
achieve	*v* (to succeed) *Finally, she **achieved** her lifelong ambition.* ➤ *n* **achievement**
acquiesce	*v* (**prep to**) (to agree reluctantly) *He was forced to **acquiesce** to their demands.* ➤ *n* **acquiescence**
acquire	*v* (to gain possession) *He **acquired** the painting during the war.* ➤ *n* **acquisition**; *adj* **acquisitive**
acrid	*adj* (sharp; bitter) *This cigar has an **acrid** taste.*
activate	*v* (to bring into use) *While she was cooking, smoke **activated** the fire alarm.* ➤ *n* **activation**

adapt	v (prep **to**) (to become suitable for different conditions) When they moved to France, they **adapted** quickly to a new house. ➤ n **adaptation**
addiction	n (prep **to**) (a powerful, often harmful, habit) His **addiction** to alcohol is getting worse. ➤ adj **addictive**; pn **addict**
address	v (to speak formally) The President **addressed** the crowd. ➤ n **address**
adept	adj (prep **at**) (capable) He was **adept** at solving problems.
adequate	adj (enough for the purpose) The money wasn't **adequate** to buy the shirt. ➤ n **adequacy**; neg **inadequate**
adhere	v (prep **to**) (to stick firmly) He always **adheres** to his principles. ➤ n **adherence**
adjacent	adj (prep **to**) (next to; adjoining) There is a parking lot **adjacent** to the shopping center.
admire	v (to think of with pleasure or respect) I **admire** your father very much.
admonish	v (prep **for**, **against**) (to warn about; to advise against doing something) The policeman **admonished** him for driving at high speed.
adolescence	n (period between childhood and maturity) The period of **adolescence** is a very important part of a teenager's development. ➤ adj **adolescent**
adore	v (to love greatly) Because of her beauty, she was **adored** by all the boys at school. ➤ n **adoration**
adroit	adj (prep **at**) (clever; skillful) Steve was very **adroit** at math and therefore decided to study it at university.
adult	adj (mature) Now that he's twenty-one, he should behave in a more **adult** way. ➤ pn **adult**
adulterate	v (prep **with**) (to spoil by adding something) The beer was **adulterated** with water. ➤ n **adulteration**
adverse	adj (prep **to**) (opposing) They were **adverse** to change and only approved the original contract.
advocate	pn (a person who speaks in defense of someone or something) His **advocate** advised him to tell the whole truth. ➤ v **advocate**
affect	v (influence; to cause some result or change) The strike by the miners **affected** the price of coal. ➤ n **affect**; adj **affective**

affiliate	*v* (*prep* **with, to**) (to join or connect especially to a larger group) *Our club was **affiliated** to a national organization.* ➤ n **affiliation**
affliction	*n* (that which causes suffering or unhappiness) *The spots on her face were a long-lasting **affliction**.* ➤ v **afflict** (*prep* **with, by**)
affluent	*adj* (rich, wealthy) *Because he was very rich, he lived in the most **affluent** neighborhood in the town.* ➤ n **affluence**
aftermath	*n* (*prep* **of**) (period after a bad event) *The **aftermath** of the war was very tense.*
aggravate	*v* (to make worse) *The lack of rain in Ethiopia **aggravated** the crisis caused by the civil war.* ➤ n **aggravation**
aggressive	*adj* (*prep* **toward, to**) (ready to attack or quarrel) *He was very **aggressive** toward his brother.* ➤ n **aggression**; *pn* **aggressor**
agile	*adj* (able to move quickly and easily) *To be an acrobat you must be very **agile**.* ➤ n **agility**
agitate	*v* (to become anxious or nervous) *He became very **agitated** when he could not solve a problem.* ➤ n **agitation**
aglow	*adj* (*prep* **with**) (bright with color or excitement) *His face was **aglow** with excitement.*
ailment	*n* (a mild illness) *The woman visited the doctor with a new **ailment** every week.* ➤ v **ail**
ajar	*adj* (slightly open) *I left the door **ajar** so that I could hear the doorbell ring.*
akin	*adj* (*prep* **to**) (similar; having the same character or nature) *His responsibilities at work are roughly **akin** to mine.*
alert	*adj* (*prep* **to**) (watchful and ready to deal with danger; vigilant) *While traveling he is always **alert** to thieves.* ➤ n **alertness**
alienate	*v* (*prep* **from**) (to make someone feel as if they do not belong) *He felt **alienated** from society.* ➤ n **alienation**
allege	*v* (to state or declare without proof) *The newspaper **alleged** that the senator had an affair.* ➤ n **allegation** (*prep* **of**)
allegiance	*n* (*prep* **to**) (loyalty, fidelity to a leader, country, ideal) *They had to swear **allegiance** to the flag.*
alleviate	*v* (to lessen; to relieve) *The pills the nurse gave him helped to **alleviate** the pain.* ➤ n **alleviation**
allocate	*v* (*prep* **to, for**) (to set apart for a particular purpose, to earmark) *The government **allocated** over $100 million to the hospital.* ➤ n **allocation**

allude	v (prep **to**) (to speak of something in an indirect way) She didn't mention his name but it was obvious she was **alluding** to him. ➤ n **allusion**
alluring	adj (attractive, charming) She looked very **alluring** in her new red dress. ➤ n **allure**
aloof	adj (prep **toward, to**) (reserved; indifferent) Since winning the lottery she's been very **aloof** towards her old friends. ➤ n **aloofness**
alter	v (to make or become different) It was clear from his uncharacteristic silence that he was much **altered** by the experience. ➤ n **alteration**
amalgamate	v (prep **with**) (to join to make larger, combine) The chemical division of the company was **amalgamated** with the mineral division. ➤ n **amalgamation**
ambiguous	adj (having more than one meaning, unclear) He gave me an **ambiguous** answer, so I still didn't understand. ➤ n **ambiguity**
ambivalent	adj (prep **toward, about**) (having opposing feelings or opinion) Despite all her attempts to persuade him, he remained **ambivalent**. ➤ n **ambivalence**
ameliorate	v (improve; lessen) His bad mood was **ameliorated** by the prize he received. ➤ n **amelioration**
amend	v (to make changes in a rule of law) After 1958, criminal law was **amended**. ➤ n **amendment**
amenities	n (something in a town, hotel, etc. that provides enjoyment; facilities) The park and the bowling club are the town's main **amenities**.
amicable	adj (friendly) After months of negotiations we reached an **amicable** agreement.
amnesia	n (a loss of memory) As the result of a car crash she suffered from temporary **amnesia**.
ample	adj (adequate; enough) They had **ample** time in which to finish the test.
amplify	v (to make larger and more powerful; expand) He needed a microphone to **amplify** his voice because people at the back couldn't hear him. ➤ n **amplification**
ancestor	pn (a person from whom one is descended) In order to write the family tree she had to find out who her **ancestors** were. ➤ n **ancestry**; adj **ancestral**
anguish	n (great pain especially of the mind) He suffered great **anguish** over his wife's death.
animate	v (to give life or excitement to) He became **animated** when he saw her. ➤ n **animation**

animosity   *n* (*prep* **to, toward**) (hostility) He felt much **animosity** toward his boss when he was passed over for promotion.

annual   *adj* (yearly)
His **annual** salary is twice as big as mine.

anomalous   *adj* (irregular) The doctors were puzzled because of the **anomalous** form of the cancer.

anonymous   *adj* (unnamed, unknown) She received a letter from an **anonymous** admirer. ➤ *n* **anonymity**

antagonize   *v* (to cause to become an enemy or opponent) He was **antagonized** by her constant demands for money. ➤ *n* **antagonism**; *adj* **antagonistic**; *adv* **antagonistically**

anticipate   *v* (to expect/guess in advance) She tried to **anticipate** what they would ask her during the interview. ➤ *n* **anticipation** (*prep* **of**)

apocalyptic   *adj* (prediction of great disaster) Many believed the first atom bomb explosion would be **apocalyptic**. ➤ *n* **apocalypse**

appoint   *v* (*prep* **to, as**) (to choose for a position or job) He was **appointed** to the position of managing director. ➤ *n* **appointment**

appraisal   *n* (*prep* **of**) (a valuation) Each year the company conducts an **appraisal** of its performance.

appropriate   *v* (to take for oneself) It was discovered that one of the directors had **appropriated** the company's money.

arduous   *adj* (demanding great effort; strenuous) His job in the factory was dirty and **arduous**.

aromatic   *adj* (having a nice smell) She added some **aromatic** herbs to the casserole. ➤ *n* **aroma**

arouse   *v* (to cause to become active) His strange behavior **aroused** the teacher's suspicions. ➤ *n* **arousal**

arraign   *v* (*prep* **with, for**) (to charge; to accuse) The police decided to **arraign** him with grand larceny.

array   *v* (to set in order) The glasses on the shelf were **arrayed** in a row. ➤ *n* **array** (*prep* **of**)

arrogance   *n* (haughtiness, great pride) After he obtained his Ph.D., his **arrogance** put everybody off. ➤ *adj* **arrogant**

artificial   *adj* (not genuine; made by human) This drink doesn't contain any **artificial** coloring. ➤ *n* **artificiality**

aspire   *v* (*prep* **to**) (to strive toward; to seek eagerly) Even as a young girl she **aspired** to be a teacher. ➤ *n* **aspiration**

assert	*v* (to affirm an opinion) *Although nobody believed her, she continued to **assert** her innocence.* ➤ n **assertion**; *adj* **assertive**
asset	*n* (*prep* **of**) (a useful or valuable quality; finances) *The company has **assets** of over $100,000.*
assimilate	*v* (*prep* **to**, **into**) (to take in, to absorb into) *They were **assimilated** quickly into their new environment.* ➤ n **assimilation**
associate	*v* (*prep* **with**) (to connect; relate to) *The changing weather has been **associated** with global warming.* ➤ n **association**
assuage	*v* (to ease; to lessen) *He **assuaged** his thirst by drinking a whole bottle of Coca-Cola.*
assume	*v* (to begin to have; to take) *After the riots the army **assumed** control of the region.* ➤ n **assumption** (*prep* **of**)
astound	*v* (to surprise greatly; to astonish) *He was **astounded** by his unexpected test results.*
astray	*adv* (away from the correct path or direction) *It was the older boys who led the child **astray** causing him to end up in juvenile court.*
attain	*v* (to gain) *After ten years he **attained** the position of managing director.* ➤ n **attainment** (*prep* **of**)
attract	*v* (to get attention) *The swimmer managed to **attract** the attention of the lifeguard.* ➤ n **attraction** (*prep* **to**)
attribute	*v* (*prep* **to**) (to be explained by) *His success was **attributed** to hard work.*
attrition	*n* (slowly weakening and wearing down) *Because both sides in the war were unable to achieve a clear military superiority it turned into a war of **attrition**.*
audacious	*adj* (daring) *The **audacious** attempt to rescue the injured pilot was successful.* ➤ n **audacity**
audible	*adj* (able to be heard) *He spoke so softly that his voice was barely **audible** at the back of the hall.* ➤ n **audibility**
augment	*v* (to increase) *She **augments** her income by giving private lessons.*
authenticate	*v* (to prove to be true or genuine) *The police were able to **authenticate** the suspect's alibi.* ➤ *adj* **authentic**
autonomous	*adj* (self governing; independent) *Monaco is an **autonomous** state.* ➤ n **autonomy**
avarice	*n* (extreme desire to get or keep wealth) *She was notorious for her **avarice** and took every cent she could from her husband.* ➤ *adj* **avaricious**

aversion   *n* **(prep to)** (intense dislike) *He has an* **aversion** *to getting up early.*

award   *v* (to give something earned or deserved) *He was* **awarded** *$100 as the first prize.*

B

baffle   *v* (to confuse) He was **baffled** by the problem.

bald   *adj* (without hair) As a young man his hair was very thick, but when he reached his fifties he began to go **bald**. ➤ *n* **baldness**

ban   *v* (*prep* **from**) (to declare that something must not be done; to prohibit) He was **banned** from driving.

bankruptcy   *n* (a state of economic ruin) After the bank refused the loan, the company was on the verge of **bankruptcy**. ➤ *adj* **bankrupt**

baptize   *v* (*prep* **as**) (to give a name) The press **baptized** the new political campaign a disaster. ➤ *n* **baptism**

bar   *n* (the profession of law) After years of studying law he was finally called to the **bar**.

barricade   *n* (a barrier; an obstruction) To stop the tanks, the revolutionaries put up **barricades**. ➤ *v* **barricade**

beckon   *v* (to summon with a signal from the hand) She **beckoned** them into her office.

bellow   *v* (to shout loudly) The sergeant **bellowed** the order to his troops. ➤ *n* **bellow**

beneficiary   *n* (a person who receives money or property from an insurance policy or will) The millionaire's wife was the sole **beneficiary** of his will.

benign   *adj* (harmless) He was relieved to hear the cancer was **benign**.

beset   *v* (*prep* **by, with**) (to attack continuously) He was **beset** by worries about his health.

betray   *v* (to give information to an enemy) The traitor **betrayed** the names of CIA agents. ➤ *n* **betrayal**

beverage   *n* (a liquid (though not water) for drinking) The laws concerning the sale of alcoholic **beverages** vary from state to state.

bewilder   v (to confuse) Doctors remain **bewildered** by the speed with which the epidemic has spread. ➤ n **bewilderment**

bicker   v (to argue in a petty way) The president advised the senators not to **bicker** over details but to support the proposal.

bind   v (prep **to**) (to join) He wanted to leave the company but he was **bound** to them by contract.

blandishment   n (coaxing; persuasion by flattery) Despite the **blandishments** of his boss, he refused to take the new job.

bleak   adj (cold and bare; cheerless) The prospects were so **bleak** that the company was forced to declare bankruptcy.

blend   v (prep **with**) (to mix) To obtain the color they wanted, it was necessary to **blend** several shades of paint.

blunder   n (an error; a mistake) It is now clear that the decision not to join the union was a **blunder**. ➤ v to blunder

bonanza   n (a commercial success; an abundance) The company's decision to invest in the idea proved a **bonanza**.

boom   n (business expansion) The discovery of oil in the state led to a massive economic **boom**.

boost   v (to increase, raise)
News of the takeover **boosted** profits.

boundless   adj (without limits) His success is due to his **boundless** energy.

brandish   v (to shake or wave something) When he **brandished** the knife she ran away.

brawl   n (a noisy fight or quarrel) The **brawl** between the drunks was so noisy that the police had to be called. ➤ v **brawl**

bribe   n (money or a gift used to influence) The student offered a **bribe** to the teacher for a look at the exam questions. ➤ v **bribe**

brink   n (at the edge of a steep drop) The directors were on the **brink** of hiring him when they discovered his criminal past.

brittle   adj (easily broken) After being buried for thousands of years, the iron arrow-head was extremely **brittle**.

brutal   adj (savage; cruel) The terrorists were known to be **brutal** men who often shot their prisoners. ➤ n **brutality**

bully   v (to persuade with threats) The salesman was so aggressive that he **bullied** customers to buy. ➤ pn **bully**

burrow   v (prep **under, into, through**) (to dig under the surface) The soldiers **burrowed** deep into the hillside.

bylaw   n (a local regulation, element of law) One of the **bylaws** of the park prohibits kissing.

C

calculate — *v* (to estimate) He **calculated** that one more tank of gas would get him home. ➤ *n* **calculation**

callous — *adj* (insensitive; unfeeling) The crime showed the killer had a **callous** disregard for life.

candidate — *n* (an aspirant, an applicant) None of the **candidates** had any special qualities suitable to the job.

capacity — *n* (*prep* **for**) (extent of ability) Her **capacity** for work was impressive.

captivate — *v* (to retain interest) The audience were **captivated** by his skill.

carnivore — *n* (a meat eater) The lion is not the fiercest of the **carnivores**. ➤ *adj* **carnivorous**

cast — *v* (to give a role) He was **cast** as the hero of the film.

castigate — *v* (*prep* **for**) (to reprove) The ambassador **castigated** the secretary for failing to finish typing the report. ➤ *n* **castigation**

cataclysm — *n* (a terrible event) The earthquake was a **cataclysm** that destroyed cities and left millions homeless.

celebrity — *n* (a famous person) Several **celebrities** came to the show's opening night.

celestial — *adj* (of space and the stars) The first **celestial** maps were made from plotting the stars.

censure — *v* (to reprove) The committee decided to **censure** him for his frequent absences. ➤ *n* **censure**

challenge — *v* (to test ability) He needs a job that really **challenges** him.

chaos — *n* (without organization; confusion) The burglars had overturned everything and left the room in a state of **chaos**. ➤ *adj* **chaotic**

chasm — *n* (a deep crack in the ground) The **chasms** in this area were caused by glaciers during the ice age.

chaste	adj (pure) His first impression was that she was **chaste** and modest. ➤ n **chastity**
chore	n (a menial, boring job) Her **chores** involved cleaning and cooking.
circulation	n (sales of a publication) The **circulation** of the magazine has risen by fifty percent. ➤ v **circulate**
cite	v (to quote) The president **cited** the Bible many times during his speech.
clemency	n (kindness; mercy) The convicted man asked the court for **clemency** because the crime was his first offense.
clutter	v (confused; disorganized; littered) He always **cluttered** his desk with papers and reference materials.
codicil	n (a clause added to a will) A **codicil** to the will stopped the eldest inheriting any money.
coerce	v (prep **into**) (to compel by pressure or threat) The police **coerced** him into signing the confession by threatening to involve his wife. ➤ n **coercion**
cogent	adj (rational, convincing) He presented his ideas in such a **cogent** manner that no one objected. ➤ n **cogency**
cohere	v (to stick together) His arguments simply don't **cohere**. ➤ adj **coherent**; n **coherence**
collate	v (to arrange in order) The papers were in such a disorder that it took her an hour to **collate** them.
collide	v (prep **with**) (to hit something) The car was doing at least 50 mph when it **collided** with the tree. ➤ n **collision**
combat	v (to fight) New techniques and drugs will have to be found to **combat** the disease. ➤ n **combat**; adj **combative**
commemorate	v (to celebrate a memory) The new medal **commemorates** the end of the war. ➤ n **commemoration**
commend	v (to praise) The soldier was **commended** for bravery above and beyond the call of duty.
commission	v (to order a job) She was **commissioned** to write a series of text books.
compassion	n (sympathy; pity) She felt **compassion** for the people made homeless by the hurricane. ➤ adj **compassionate**
compatible	adj (prep **with**) (able to exist or work together) Environmental concern is not usually **compatible** with large company profits. ➤ n **compatibility**; neg **incompatible**
compel	v (to force) The court **compelled** the police to arrest the diplomat despite his immunity. ➤ n **compulsion**

compensate	*v* (*prep* **for, with**) (to provide payment for loss or damage) *The company had to **compensate** him for loss of earnings.* ➤ *n* **compensation**
compete	*v* (*prep* **for, with**) (to try to win) *Three companies **competed** for the contract.* ➤ *n* **competition**; *adj* **competitive**
complement	*v* (to combine well, to form a whole) *A further six lectures are planned to **complement** the course.*
complexion	*n* (the natural color and appearance of skin) *Her **complexion** is so flawless that she seldom wears makeup.*
compliment	*v* (*prep* **for, on**) (to express admiration) *The director **complimented** him on the new design.* ➤ *adj* **complimentary**
comply	*v* (*prep* **with**) (to obey) *Employees are expected to **comply** with all company regulations.*
component	*n* (*prep* **of**) (part of something) *One small **component** of the engine was found to be faulty.*
comprehensive	*adj* (including everything) *The committee ordered that a **comprehensive** plan should be prepared.*
compress	*v* (*prep* **into**) (to reduce in size, force into a smaller space) *Lacking paper, he was forced to **compress** his composition into two pages.* ➤ *n* **compression**; *prep* **into**
compulsory	*adj* (obligatory, required by the rules) *It is **compulsory** for all students to attend statistics lectures.* ➤ *v* **compel**
conceal	*v* (to hide) *She tried to **conceal** her identity by using a false passport.* ➤ *n* **concealment**
conceit	*n* (to have a high opinion of oneself) *However intelligent, he was too **conceited** to have as a friend.*
concise	*adj* (of speech or writing, short, brief but complete) *A good sentence should contain all the information yet be **concise**.*
concoct	*v* (to devise; to invent) *To explain his absence, he **concocted** an excuse.* ➤ *n* **concoction** (*prep* **of**)
concord	*n* (harmony) *Despite differences of race, they lived in **concord**.*
concur	*v* (*prep* **with**) (to agree) *The board of directors **concurred** with the findings of the advisory committee.* ➤ *n* **concurrence**
condone	*v* (to overlook; to excuse) *Although I approve of his goals, I can no longer **condone** his activities.*
conducive	*adj* (*prep* **to**) (helping) *The noise from the stereo wasn't **conducive** to study.*

confide	v (prep **to, in**) (to entrust a secret) *As a schoolboy, he always **confided** his problems to his best friend.* ➤ pn **confidant**
confident	adj (sure of oneself) *He was so **confident** of his abilities that he rarely rehearsed before a concert.* ➤ n **confidence**
confine	v (to keep in a restricted space) *The soldier was **confined** to camp until he could be sent home.* ➤ n **confinement**
confiscate	v (to seize by authority) *The police **confiscated** all the documents relating to the transaction.* ➤ n **confiscation** (prep **of**)
conflict	v (prep **with**) (to oppose or disagree) *His statement **conflicted** with those of other witnesses.* ➤ n **conflict**
congeal	v (to become hard; to solidify) *By the time he reached the hospital, the stream of blood had begun to **congeal**.*
congenial	adj (pleasant; suited to one's taste; agreeable) *At first sight the room looked comfortable and **congenial**.*
congenital	adj (existing at birth) *Following its birth, the baby was found to have a **congenital** disease.*
congestion	n (crowding) *With the main road closed, the traffic **congestion** has become unbearable.*
conjecture	n (a supposition; a guess) *His idea is just a **conjecture** and cannot be relied upon.*
conscientious	adj (careful; honest) *He may not be very smart but at least he's a very **conscientious** worker.* ➤ n **conscience**
consecutive	adj (following each other) *The bills were numbered in **consecutive** order so they were easy to trace.*
consequences	n (prep **of**) (results) *She hadn't thought about the **consequences** of her actions.* ➤ adj **consequential**
consistent	adj (prep **with**) (in agreement; unchanging) *Stealing the money is totally **consistent** with his character.*
console	v (to offer sympathy) *She tried to **console** her daughter after her pony died.* ➤ n **consolation**
conspicuous	adj (clearly noticeable) *Wearing a bright red hat, he was a very **conspicuous** character.*
conspire	v (prep **with, to**) (to plan with others) *They **conspired** to shoot the president on his birthday.* ➤ n **conspiracy**
constituent	n (part of the whole) *She kept the recipe secret but he knew the main **constituent** was milk.* ➤ v **constitute**
constrain	v (to hold back) *The detective managed to **constrain** the prisoner by slipping handcuffs on his wrists.* ➤ n **constraint**
construe	v (to understand an implication) *He **construed** her silence to mean that she was willing.*

consume	*v* (to use up) *The task **consumed** his whole evening.* ➤ *n* **consumption**
contaminate	*v* (to pollute) *The discharge from the factory **contaminated** a five mile stretch of the river.* ➤ *n* **contamination**
contemporary	*adj* (of the same time) *She found it was easier to relate to **contemporary** writers than those of the 19th century.*
contiguous	*adj* **(prep to, with)** (next to in time or order; adjacent) *The outbreak of the war was **contiguous** to the failure of the peace talks.*
contract	*v* (to reduce) *Metal **contracts** as it cools.* ➤ *n* **contraction**
contribute	*v* **(prep to)** (to give) *Members of the club **contributed** ten per cent of their annual earnings to charity.* ➤ *n* **contribution**
contrive	*v* (to cause something to happen) *He had no idea that she had **contrived** their meeting.* ➤ *n* **contrivance**
controversial	*adj* (causing argument) *The decision to legalize abortion was very **controversial**.* ➤ *n* **controversy**
convey	*v* **(prep to)** (to carry) *Please could you **convey** to him my best wishes.*
convict	*v* **(prep of)** (to find guilty) *The bank manager was finally **convicted** of fraud.* ➤ *n* **conviction**
convulsion	*n* (violent, uncontrollable shaking) *He thought he'd been cured of malaria until the **convulsions** began.*
copious	*adj* (abundant, profuse) *Throughout the lecture he took **copious** notes.*
core	*n* **(prep of)** (the center) *His desire for power was at the **core** of the problem.*
counteract	*v* (to oppose by opposite action) *They found that the drug **counteracted** many of the symptoms of the disease.* ➤ *n* **counteraction**
counterfeit	*adj* (false) *The bank clerk was shocked to find that most of the bank notes were **counterfeit**.* ➤ *pn* **counterfeiter**
crave	*v* (to desire greatly) *Even as a young man he had **craved** fame.*
credulous	*adj* (inclined to believe too readily; gullible) *The official was far too **credulous** and believed the most unlikely stories.*
creed	*n* (a belief; a faith) *According to the constitution, all Americans regardless of race or **creed** are equal.*
crude	*adj* (not finished; rough) *The painting was still in a **crude** state but he recognized her features.* ➤ *n* **crudity**
cruise	*v* (to drive slowly) *On Sunday evenings the family used to **cruise** around town in their beloved car.*

crumb   *n* (a small piece) *You don't have a **crumb** of evidence to support that idea.*

cryptic   *adj* (secret; hidden) *Instead of being so **cryptic**, tell me what you really think.* ➤ *v* **encrypt**

culmination   *n* (the conclusion) *His appointment as manager came as the **culmination** of years of hard work.* ➤ *v* **culminate** (*prep* **in**)

culpable   *adj* (*prep* **of**) (deserving blame) *After the patient's death the doctor was found **culpable** of neglect.* ➤ *n* **culpability**

curb   *v* (to limit) *Unless he **curbs** his drinking, he'll be dead by this time next year.*

curriculum   *n* (contents of a course of study) *The **curriculum** covered only modern American history.*

curt   *adj* (rudely brief in speech or manner) *She complained to the manager that the shop assistant had been **curt** and offensive.*

curtail   *v* (to shorten; to suspend) *Because of the weather, even the train services had to be **curtailed**.*

D

dalliance   *n* (a trivial occupation) *Generally, fox hunting is a **dalliance** of the rich and idle.*

dangle   *v* (to hang loosely) *They **dangled** their fishing lines in the water for hours without catching a single fish.*

deadline   *n* (last possible time to deliver something) *He had to work all through the night to finish the paper before the **deadline**.*

debt   *n* (what is owed) *To buy the car he had to borrow and got into **debt**.* ➤ *pn* **debtor**

decadent   *adj* (without morals) *Authority broke down and the country became **decadent**.* ➤ *n* **decadence**

deception   *n* (something which is false, but is made to seem true) *They used false money to create the **deception**.* ➤ *v* **deceive**

decline   *n* (a downward slope; a decrease) *Without any industries left, the neighborhood began to **decline** socially.*

decode   *v* (to break a code) *The Americans managed to **decode** the message and learned the secrets of the enemy.*

decrepit   *adj* (weakened by illness or age) *The trains are in a **decrepit** condition but the rail company can't afford to buy new ones.*

dedicate   *v* (prep **to**) (to devote to, to concentrate on) *After the accident, he **dedicated** himself to research.* ➤ *n* **dedication**

deduce   *v* (to solve by reason) *He **deduced** from the ash that the killer was a smoker.* ➤ *n* **deduction**

deed   *n* (an act) *The millionaire was known for his good **deeds** for charity.*

deem   *v* (to judge) *He was promoted because the director **deemed** him worthy of the position.*

defect   *n* (an imperfection) *Because of a **defect** in the engine, he returned the car.* ➤ *adj* **defective**

deficiency   *n* (a lack) *The doctor blamed his ill heath on a **deficiency** in his diet.* ➤ *adj* **deficient**

deformed   *adj* (disfigured) *His leg had been* **deformed** *since birth.* ➤ *n* **deformity**

defray   *v* (bear the cost of, pay for) *The company sought outside investors to* **defray** *the costs of the project.*

delegate   *n* (representative) *The first congress decided to send three* **delegates** *to the Washington conference.*

demolish   *v* (to destroy completely) *The house was* **demolished** *to make way for the new road.*

demote   *v* (*prep* **to**) (to lower in rank) *As a result of the offense, the soldier was* **demoted** *to corporal.* ➤ *n* **demotion**

denote   *v* (to signify) *He wore a special badge to* **denote** *his position in the company.*

dent   *n* (*prep* **in, to**) (a depression) *The only sign of the crash he could find was a small* **dent** *in the side door.* ➤ *v* **dent**

depict   *v* (to describe, show) *The movie* **depicts** *life in the USA today.* ➤ *n* **depiction**

deplete   *v* (to reduce quantity) *After three months of drought, the water in the reservoir had been greatly* **depleted.** ➤ *n* **depletion**

deprecate   *v* (to express disapproval) *We feel that we must* **deprecate** *such an act of savage aggression.* ➤ *adj* **deprecatory**

deprive   *v* (*prep* **of**) (to take away) *The loss of his leg* **deprived** *him of his profession.* ➤ *n* **deprivation**

deregulate   *v* (to cancel regulation) *The government decided to* **deregulate** *the entire telecommunication industry to stimulate faster growth.*

deride   *v* (to make fun of; to jeer) *The other boys* **derided** *him because of his funny accent.* ➤ *n* **derision**; *adj* **derisive**

derive   *v* (*prep* **from**) (to extract from) *Steel is* **derived** *from iron ore.* ➤ *n* **derivation, derivative**

designate   *v* (to name; to specify) *He* **designated** *his closest friends as directors of the company.* ➤ *n* **designation**

detect   *v* (to discover) *The radar operator* **detected** *a faint signal from the aircraft.* ➤ *n* **detection**

deter   *v* (to discourage) *To* **deter** *further robberies, he kept a gun in his desk.* ➤ *n* **deterrent**

deterioration   *n* (becoming worse) *Overnight, there was a marked* **deterioration** *in his health and by the next morning he was dead.* ➤ *v* **deteriorate**

detest   *v* (to hate) *At first he was just annoyed by her but eventually he grew to* **detest** *her.*

detract	*v* (*prep* **from**) (to harm by taking away) *The new suspension bridge greatly **detracts** from the view.*
detrimental	*adj* (harmful) *It has been proved that cigarettes are **detrimental** to your health.*
devastate	*v* (to destroy) *The entire region was **devastated** by the hurricane.*
deviate	*v* (*prep* **from**) (to depart from; to differ) *The discussion **deviated** from the planned subject matter.* ➤ n **deviation**
devise	*v* (to invent) *The scientist **devised** a completely new instrument to complete the task.* ➤ n **device**
devoid	*adj* (*prep* **of**) (empty) *It was clear from the space probe that Mars was **devoid** of life.*
diffidence	*n* (lack of confidence) *Although she displays **diffidence** with strangers she is very self-confident with friends.*
digress	*v* (*prep* **from**) (to stray from the main subject) *The speaker frequently **digressed** from the subject.* ➤ n **digression**
dilate	*v* (to become wider and larger) *Under hypnosis, the pupils of his eyes became **dilated**.*
diligent	*adj* (industrious; careful) *She proved a very **diligent** secretary and always stayed late at the office.* ➤ n **diligence**
diminish	*v* (to get less) *After an hour in the casino his money had greatly **diminished**.*
diminutive	*adj* (very small, tiny) *Her **diminutive** stature was due to a gene deficiency.*
dingy	*adj* (dirty; shabby) *He lived in a **dingy** room because he couldn't afford anything better.*
disband	*v* (to dissolve; to discontinue) *Following its electoral defeat the party was **disbanded**.*
discard	*v* (to throw out) *Having **discarded** the other options, she decided to accept the offer.*
discern	*v* (to recognize; to perceive) *In the half light, she could just about **discern** a small hut at the edge of the field.*
disclosure	*n* (something revealed) *His fans were shocked by the **disclosure** that he was married.* ➤ v **disclose**
discount	*v* (to dismiss as unimportant or untrue) *He decided to **discount** the rumors of danger and continue with the mission.*
disintegrate	*v* (to fall apart) *Her confidence **disintegrated** when she examined the test paper.* ➤ n **disintegration**
dismal	*adj* (miserable) *The weather was **dismal** with howling winds and steady rain.*
disobedience	*n* (a refusal to follow orders) *He was thrown out of the army for **disobedience**.* ➤ v **disobey**

dispatch   *v* (to send) *The entire amount was packed and **dispatched** by nightfall.* ➤ *pn* **dispatcher**

dispense   *v* (*prep* **with**) (to do without) *I think we can **dispense** with formalities and get straight to business.*

disperse   *v* (to scatter) *After the meeting, the delegates **dispersed** back to their homes.* ➤ *n* **dispersal**

displace   *v* (to move from home or place) *Thousands of refugees have been **displaced** from their homes.*

dispute   *v* (to argue) *He accepted the need for change but **disputed** the means to achieve it.* ➤ *n* **dispute**

dissect   *v* (to analyze; to criticize in great detail) *The examiners **dissected** every sentence of his essay.* ➤ *n* **dissection**

disseminate   *v* (to spread; to distribute) *News of the peace agreement was disseminated internationally by television satellites.* ➤ *n* **dissemination**

dissipate   *v* (to cause to disappear) *With the help of drugs, the symptoms quickly **dissipated**.*

distill   *v* (to extract the essence) *The critic had managed to **distill** the most important elements from the book.*

distinguish   *v* (to differentiate) *She was **distinguished** from her classmates by her great musical talent.*

distort   *v* (to alter the shape or meaning) *In the desert, the view of the horizon is frequently **distorted** by the heat.* ➤ *n* **distortion**

diverse   *adj* (varied) *He had **diverse** reasons for taking up singing but mainly it was to earn money.* ➤ *n* **diversification**; *v* **diversify**

divert   *v* (to entertain; to amuse) *Throughout the bombing raid, the children in the shelter were **diverted** with games.*

divulge   *v* (to make known; to reveal) *The prisoner was tortured until he **divulged** the hiding place of his comrades.*

doze   *v* (to sleep for a short time) *Several passengers were still **dozing** when the train pulled into the station.*

draft   *adj* (an initial version) *It was clear from the first **draft** of the report that it would be controversial.*

drench   *v* (to make very wet) *They were **drenched** by the sudden downpour.*

drought   *n* (a long period of dry weather) *The water level in the reservoir was dangerously low because of the long **drought**.*

dubious   *adj* (*prep* **about, of**) (doubtful) *Most reporters were **dubious** about the story but decided it had to be printed.*

duplicate   *v* (to copy) He **duplicated** the experiment exactly but the results differed.

durable   *adj* (sturdy; lasting) The tests proved that the plastic tires were more **durable** than those of rubber. ➤ n **durability**

dusk   *n* (just before night) The fireworks display will begin at **dusk**.

dwell   *v* (*prep* **in, at**) (to reside, inhabit) He was forced to **dwell** for the entire winter in a cardboard box. ➤ n **dwelling**

dwindle   *v* (to lessen) Stocks of fuel were **dwindling** as the temperature remained close to zero.

dye   *v* (to color) She tried to **dye** her hair green.

E

earmark   *v* (to allocate in advance) *The council voted to **earmark** ten per cent of the expected income to finance the project.*

eavesdrop   *v* (*prep* **on**) (to overhear secretly) *Microphones were hidden in the room to **eavesdrop** on the robbers.*

eccentric   *adj* (strange; odd) *She looks very **eccentric** wearing those purple socks.* ➤ *n* **eccentricity**

effect   *v* (to cause to happen) *It was the introduction of the five day week that **effected** the greatest change.* ➤ *n* **effect**

eject   *v* (*prep* **from**) (to throw or force out, expel) *The pilot managed to **eject** safely from the doomed jet.* ➤ *n* **ejection**

eligible   *adj* (to be qualified to do something) *Only men who have completed military service are **eligible** to vote.* ➤ *n* **eligibility**

eloquence   *n* (persuasive and graceful language) *The politician's **eloquence** was admired even by his enemies.* ➤ *adj* **eloquent**

elucidate   *v* (to make understandable) *The more he tried to **elucidate** his ideas the more he confused the audience.*

elusive   *adj* (tending to escape notice) *The terrorists proved so **elusive** that it was months before the FBI caught up with them.*

emaciated   *adj* (very thin and under-nourished) *After two years in the prison camp, all the survivors were **emaciated** and barely alive.*

emancipate   *v* (to set free) *The slaves were legally **emancipated** a year after the war.* ➤ *n* **emancipation** (*prep* **of**)

emerge   *v* (*prep* **from**) (to come out) *When he **emerged** from prison, he was a changed man.* ➤ *n* **emergence**

emit   *v* (*prep* **from, by**) (to give off) *Radiation was **emitted** from the nuclear reaction.* ➤ *n* **emission**

emphasis   *n* (*prep* **on**) (special attention) *The **emphasis** was on theory rather than practice.* ➤ *v* **emphasize**

emulate   *v* (to try to equal) *Unconsciously he tried to **emulate** the literary style of his father.*

encapsulate	*v* (to include or condense) *The course **encapsulated** all of Freud's main theories.*
encounter	*v* (to meet) *On the journey she **encountered** many dangers.* ➤ *n* **encounter**
encroach	*v* (*prep* **on, upon**) (to take more than is right) *His duties have begun to **encroach** upon mine.*
endeavor	*v* (to make an effort; to try very hard) *He was always successful in everything he **endeavored** to do.*
endorse	*v* (to express approval or support) *When the president **endorsed** him, his chances of being elected rose.* ➤ *n* **endorsement**
enhance	*v* (to make greater and better) *Her new hair style greatly **enhanced** her beauty.* ➤ *n* **enhancement**
ensue	*v* (to follow) *The argument was about nothing important, but a serious fight **ensued**.*
entail	*v* (to involve) *Making a cake **entails** imagination as well as simply following the recipe.*
entice	*v* (to attract; to lure) *It was the smell of her perfume that **enticed** him to follow her.*
entity	*n* (the whole) *The unification of Germany has created a new political **entity**.* ➤ *adj* **entire**
envious	*adj* (*prep* **of**) (jealous) *He was very **envious** of her when he saw her brand new car.* ➤ *n* **envy**; *v* **envy**
envision	*v* (to imagine) *From the moment he first saw the site he was able to **envision** the potential it had.*
equitably	*adv* (fairly; justly) *They both received half the property and their argument was settled **equitably**.*
equivocal	*adj* (ambiguous; evasive) *Her manner is so **equivocal** that it's very hard to guess what she's thinking.*
eradicate	*v* (to remove all traces) *The new drug is able to **eradicate** the cancer completely.*
erect	*v* (to build) *The skyscraper was **erected** in record time thanks to the new technology.*
erosion	*n* (wearing away) *Strip mining has caused far more **erosion** than the logging of the rain forests.* ➤ *v* **erode**
erratic	*adj* (unpredictable) *His course attendance was **erratic** so he missed many lectures.*
erudite	*adj* (learned) *At heart she was quite simple and he was too **erudite** for her tastes.*
esteem	*n* (a favorable opinion) *He rose in her **esteem** when he turned up with flowers.*

eternal	adj (for ever) The statue is an **eternal** symbol of liberty. ➤ n **eternity**
ethnic	adj (influenced by racial origins) The city had a very wide **ethnic** mix. ➤ n **ethnicity**
eulogy	n (high praise) In his **eulogy**, he reminded those at the funeral of his father's achievements. ➤ v **eulogize**
evoke	v (to capture a feeling of) The portrait **evoked** her inner sadness. ➤ n **evocation** (prep **of**); adj **evocative**
evolve	v (to develop gradually) According to Darwin's theory humans have **evolved** from lower animals. ➤ n **evolution**
exacerbate	v (to make worse) Being forced to carry such a heavy load as he marched under the scorching sun **exacerbated** his thirst.
exacting	adj (requiring great effort) Following the money from bank to bank proved an **exacting** task.
exasperate	v (to make angry and impatient) She was **exasperated** to discover the library was closed that day. ➤ n **exasperation**
exceed	v (to be greater than) This year's profits have **exceeded** our expectations. ➤ n **excess**; adj **excessive**
exclude	v (prep **from**) (to keep out) All items worth more than a hunderd dollars were **excluded** from the sale. ➤ n **exclusion**; adj **exclusive**
execute	v (to carry out a task) The lawyers were asked to **execute** the paperwork for the project. ➤ n **execution**; adj **executive**; pn **executive**
exemplify	v (to be the best example) His warmth and wisdom **exemplified** everything a president should be. ➤ adj **exemplary**
exhausted	adj (very tired; enervated) The runners were **exhausted** after the marathon. ➤ n **exhaustion**
exorbitant	adj (extravagant; excessive) He would have liked to continue studying but thought the college fees were **exorbitant**.
expand	v (to make larger) As the temperature rose, the air in the jar **expanded**. ➤ n **expansion**; adj **expansive**
expanse	n (a large area) The desert seemed a vast **expanse** of monotonous sand dunes.
expire	v (to cease to be effective; to terminate). My driver's license will **expire** next year.
explicit	adj (very clear; definite) The instructions for the new washing machine were very **explicit** but he still couldn't work it.

exploit   *v* (to use for selfish advantage or profit) *The revolutionaries accused him of **exploiting** his workers.* ➤ n **exploit**

expound   *v (prep **on**, **upon**)* (to explain in detail) *The professor **expounded** for hours on the theory, giving numerous examples of its applications.*

extempore   *adj* (without preparation; impromptu) *I've left my notes at home so my lecture will have to be **extempore**.*

extensive   *adj* (far-reaching) *The earthquake caused **extensive** damage to the entire region.* ➤ v **extend**

extinct   *adj* (no longer active; having died out) *Despite the efforts of many environmental groups, the batwing eagle is almost **extinct**.* ➤ n **extinction**

extol   *v* (to praise highly) *In his book he **extolled** the advantages of the new system.*

extravagance   *n* (excess spending) *The recession has made long holidays an **extravagance**.* ➤ adj **extravagant**

exultant   *adj* (very happy; full of joy) *Having read the letter of acceptance by the university, he gave an **exultant** shout.*

F

facile   adj (easy, superficial) The argument he gave was too **facile** to be taken seriously.

falter   v (to move hesitatingly; unsteadily) On his way from his cell to the electric chair, he **faltered** and almost fell.

famine   n (extreme scarcity of food) The **famine** that killed more than a million people in Ireland was mainly caused by a disease in the potato crop.

fascinate   v (to attract powerfully; to charm) He was **fascinated** by her smile. ➤ n **fascination**

fastidious   adj (prep **about**) (fussy about things and appearances) He's so **fastidious** about eating that it takes him an hour to finish a simple meal. ➤ n **fastidiousness**

fatal   adj (causing death) The accident proved **fatal** and he died without regaining consciousness. ➤ n **fatality**

feat   n (an act requiring great skill, effort, or courage) The sale of his shares was a great **feat** of money-making.

feeble   adj (lacking strength or power) The old man was too **feeble** to walk. ➤ v **enfeeble**

feedback   n (prep **to, from**) (to discuss an event after it has happened) The students asked many questions so the **feedback** from his lecture was rewarding.

felon   pn (criminal) It wasn't until after the marriage that she learned that her husband was a convicted **felon**. ➤ n **felony**

ferry   v (to carry from one place to another) During the railroad strike a bus will **ferry** passengers from the train station to the airport.

feud   v (to engage in long and bitter hostility) The commander discovered that the violence was more due to **feuding** than organized warfare. ➤ n **feud**

flamboyant   adj (eye-catching, extravagant) He shocked everybody with his **flamboyant** clothes. ➤ n **flamboyance**

flatter	*v* (to praise too much) *He won her heart by **flattering** her.* ➤ *n* **flattery**
flee	*v* (*prep* **from**) (to run away) *The thieves **fled** when they heard the siren.* ➤ *n* **flight**
flicker	*v* (to shine unsteadily) *The wind caused the candle to **flicker**.*
flimsy	*adj* (lacking solidity or strength) *The hut was so **flimsy** that it fell down in the first strong wind.*
flip	*v* (to turn over) *The men **flipped** a coin to decide who should drive.*
flounder	*v* (to move awkwardly) *He slipped on the ice and **floundered** for some moments, but did not fall.*
fluffy	*adj* (soft; airy) *She liked to sleep with soft, **fluffy** pillows.*
forage	*v* (to hunt for food) *They saw a bear **foraging** in the forest.*
forbearance	*n* (self-restraint) *One needs a lot of **forbearance** to be a TOEFL teacher.*
forbid	*v* (*prep* **from**, **to**) (to ban) *He was **forbidden** from going out at night.*
ford	*v* (to cross water at a shallow place) *He traveled down the river until he found a place to **ford** it.* ➤ *n* **ford**
foreclosure	*n* (*prep* **of**) (to demand payment of a debt) *When he couldn't pay his debts, the bank ordered the **foreclosure** of the mortgage on his shop.* ➤ *v* **foreclose**
foresee	*v* (to predict) *She **foresaw** the dangers of getting involved with someone too quickly.*
formulate	*v* (to express in a formula; create in a precise form) *He **formulated** his theories according to the results of the experiments.*
fracture	*v* (to break or crack) *He fell and **fractured** his leg on the icy pavement.*
fragrance	*n* (nice scent) *The fresh flowers gave off a pleasant **fragrance**.* ➤ *adj* **fragrant**
fraud	*n* (a deception for money or property) *He was convicted of **fraud** and sent to prison for ten years.* ➤ *v* **defraud**; *adj* **fraudulent**
fret	*n* (to worry) *She always **fretted** whenever we were late coming home from school.* ➤ *adj* **fretful**
frigid	*adj* (very cold) *The **frigid** temperatures of the Arctic, forced all the four explorers to give up the expedition.*

fringe   *adj* (additional, secondary) *Because so much extra work had to be done on the project, there were a lot of **fringe** payments.* ➤ *n* **fringe**

furnace   *n* (a very large oven, often industrial) *The **furnace** in the steel factory never goes out.*

furtive   *adj* (secret) *Peter was sent out of the exam room because he was caught casting a **furtive** glance at his friend's paper.*

futile   *adj* (useless) *Unfortunately all the efforts to rescue the workers from the burning factory proved **futile**.* ➤ *n* **futility**

G

gallantry   n (bravery) *On his return from the war, he was given a medal for his **gallantry**.* ➤ adj **gallant**

gamut   n (*prep* **of**) (the complete range) *His taste in food covers the whole **gamut** of Chinese cuisine.*

garb   n (clothing) *The actors' **garb** was similar to the style worn in sixteenth century England.*

garrison   n (a fortified place occupied by soldiers) *The **garrison** was put on standby as news of a war spread around the town.*

garrulous   adj (talkative) *Peter is so **garrulous** that it is not easy for any one to get a word in when he starts talking.*

gash   n (a deep cut) *The **gash** above her eye had to be seen by a doctor immediately.*

gauche   adj (socially inept; clumsy) *His **gauche** manner was embarrassing to both his friends and family.*

generic   adj (the characteristic of a type, or group) *The **generic** name of music like this is jazz.*

genial   adj (kindly; friendly) *John received such a **genial** welcome from his friend that he felt at home immediately.* ➤ n **geniality**

genre   n (style, type) *Most of her novels belong to the **genre** of realism.*

genuine   adj (true, not false) *The art critics could not tell whether the painting was a **genuine** Picasso.*

germinate   v (to begin to grow) *The seeds will **germinate** quickly if you plant them at the right time of the year.*

gimmick   n (trick for publicity or attention) *Giving toys away with the chocolate is just a **gimmick** to make them buy more.* ➤ adj **gimmicky**

gist   n (*prep* **of**) (the main idea) *I got the **gist** of the performance but I will have to read the play to understand it in detail.*

glib	*adj* (spoken easily but with little thought; fluent) *The salesman was such a **glib** talker that he sold her goods she did not intend to buy.* ➤ n **glibness**
glimmer	*n* (faint light) *She was very ill and there was only a **glimmer** of hope that she might recover.*
glitter	*v* (to shine with a sparkling light) *Her eyes **glittered** with tears as she struggled to control her anger.*
glossary	*n* (an explanation of special words at the end of a book) *If you do not understand some of the technical terms refer to the **glossary**.*
glow	*v* (to shine dimly) *The sky **glows** at night with the light from the city.*
grant	*n* (money given, especially by the state, for a particular purpose) *She had to work to supplement her **grant**.*
greedy	*adj* (excessively desirous of acquiring possessions; avaricious) *George is a very **greedy** man, the more money he gets the more he wants.*
grievance	*n* (a complaint) *The representative of the student union brought the student's **grievances** before the college committee.*
grope	*v* (to search blindly) *When the storm caused a power failure, they all had to **grope** around in the dark for candles.*
grouchy	*adj* (irritable) *Sue could not understand why her brother had been **grouchy** all day.* ➤ v **grouch**
grudge	*n* (prep **against**) (hard feelings; resentment) *In spite of the harsh treatment she received from her tutors, she held no **grudge** against them.*
grumble	*v* (to complain) *She is not easy to please as she always **grumbles**.*
guarantee	*n* (warranty) *He wanted a written **guarantee** that the machine was in working order.* ➤ v **guarantee**
guinea pigs	*n* (subjects of a test or experiment) *The volunteers were used as **guinea pigs** in experiments to find a new anti-AIDS drug.*
gust	*n* (a sudden rush of wind) *His hat was blown off by the sudden **gust** of wind.* ➤ adj **gusty**
gymnasium	*n* (a physical education hall) *Working out at the **gymnasium** is part of her daily routine.*

H

halt	*v* (to stop) *The traffic was **halted** by a truck that had overturned at the crossroads.* ➤ n **halt**
hamper	*v* (to cause difficulty in movement or activity) *The search was **hampered** by the appalling weather conditions.*
handy	*adj* (easily reached) *Keep your dictionaries **handy** when you write your essays.*
haphazard	*adj* (without a fixed or regular course; indifferent; disorganized) *Eve got a low mark because her paper was written in a **haphazard** way.*
harrowing	*adj* (emotionally painful) *He coped well with the **harrowing** experience of losing his father.*
harsh	*adj* (cruel) *He felt the punishment was too **harsh** for the crime he had committed.*
hasty	*adj* (done too quickly to be accurate or wise) *He was forced to make a **hasty** decision which he later regretted.* ➤ n **haste**
haughty	*adj* (arrogant; cold) *His **haughty** manner made him appear cold and unfriendly.* ➤ n **haughtiness**
haunt	*v* (to be always in the thoughts of someone) *She was **haunted** by the memory of her mother's death.*
havoc	*n* (destruction, confusion) *The fire caused **havoc** in the city centre.*
hazardous	*adj* (dangerous, risky) *He took a **hazardous** mountain road to get the patient to the hospital.* ➤ n **hazard**
hazy	*adj* (obscure; cloudy) *The **hazy** weather made us change our plans to go sunbathing on the beach.* ➤ n **haziness**
hectic	*adj* (very busy; active) *It has been so **hectic** at my workplace today that I did not have time to take a break.*
heed	*v* (to pay attention to) *Had he **heeded** my advice we would not owe so much money now.*
henceforth	*adv* (from now on) ***Henceforth** this university will observe the first week in February as International Week.*

hesitate   *v* (to pause before taking an action) *Do not **hesitate** to call me if you need more information.* ➤ *n* **hesitation**; *adj* **hesitant**

hilarious   *adj* (very funny; merry; laughable) *We laughed all the way home from the movie, it was **hilarious**.* ➤ *n* **hilarity**

hinder   *v* (*prep* **from**) (to prevent) *He was **hindered** from entering by a large woman blocking the door.* ➤ *n* **hindrance**

hinge   *n* (a joint on which a door is attached) *The door squeaks because the **hinges** need oiling.*

hint   *n* (a suggestion; a clue) *If you give me a **hint** I am sure that I can guess the answer.* ➤ *v* **hint**

hoarse   *adj* (a rough and husky sound or voice) *The cheerleaders yelled themselves **hoarse** at the football game.*

hoax   *n* (a trick) *The news that a warplane had been found on the moon proved to be a **hoax**.* ➤ *v* **hoax**

hobo   *pn* (a tramp) *The **hobo** carried all his possessions in a brown paper bag.*

hoe   *n* (a garden tool) *The gardener used a **hoe** to break up the clods of earth.* ➤ *v* **hoe**

homage   *n* (*prep* **to**) (allegiance; respect) *The entire nation paid **homage** to the dead soldiers by lowering the flag to half-mast.*

hubbub   *n* (noise; confusion) *There was such a **hubbub** in the hall that few heard the opening speech.*

humid   *adj* (damp; hot) *A tropical rain forest has a very **humid** climate.* ➤ *n* **humidity**

hypothesis   *n* (a tentative theory) *His **hypothesis** that such an engine would work was later proved true.* ➤ *adj* **hypothetical**

I

identical   *adj* (exactly the same) *The twins were **identical** and the teacher had difficulty telling them apart.*

ignorant   *adj* (without knowledge; unaware; uninformed) *The senator was so **ignorant** that he didn't even know the capital city of Turkey.* ➤ n **ignorance** (*prep* **of**)

ignore   *v* (to refuse to notice or recognize) *He tried to **ignore** the child's crying and continued the talk.*

illegitimate   *adj* (not legally recognized) *The bank stopped the loan when they discovered that his claim was **illegitimate**.* ➤ n **illegitimacy**

imitate   *v* (to copy) *The child **imitated** his father's movements so well that everybody laughed.* ➤ n **imitation** (*prep* **of**); *adj* **imitative**

imminent   *adj* (about to occur; impending) *The arrival of the train was **imminent** so she had to run to be at the station in time.* ➤ n **imminence** (*prep* **of**)

immune   *adj* (*prep* **to**) (cannot be infected) *Fortunately the nurse was naturally **immune** to the disease.* ➤ n **immunity**; *v* **immunize**

impact   *n* (shock from being hit) *The **impact** when the car hit the tree was strong enough to kill the driver instantly.*

impart   *v* (to give) *He **imparted** much information but the student remained confused.*

impartial   *adj* (not favoring one more than the other) *All agreed that the referee had been totally **impartial**.* ➤ n **impartiality**

impasse   *n* (point at which it is impossible to go further) *The peace talks hit an **impasse** and in an angry mood the minister returned home.*

impede   *v* (to obstruct) *An overturned truck **impeded** his journey and he was very late.* ➤ n **impediment**

impinge	*v* (*prep* **on, upon**) (to have an effect on something) *The recession **impinged** on his plans to expand the shop.*
implement	*v* (to begin to use) *When they fell behind in the race, the team **implemented** another strategy in order to win.* ➤ *n* **implementation**
implicate	*v* (to involve) *The thief not only confessed but also **implicated** others who had helped him.* ➤ *n* **implication**
imply	*v* (to suggest) *She didn't say anything directly but **implied** that she was tired of him.* ➤ *n* **implication**
impoverish	*v* (to make poor) *From being **impoverished** by the stock market crash, she recovered to die extremely wealthy.*
impromptu	*adj* (without preparation; unrehearsed) *Since he did not have time to prepare a talk his comments were completely **impromptu**.*
impulse	*n* (reflex, reaction) *He acted on **impulse**.* ➤ *adj* **impulsive**
inaugurate	*v* (ceremonially open) *The new office was **inaugurated** with a party.* ➤ *n* **inauguration** (*prep* **of**)
incessant	*adj* (without interruption; continuous) *The **incessant** noise of the passing trains kept him awake all night.*
incidence	*n* (frequency) *The **incidence** of gun crimes is going up all the time.*
incidental	*adj* (of lesser importance; secondary) *There was an extra charge to cover **incidental** expenses.*
incision	*n* (a cut into something) *The surgeon was so expert that the scar from the **incision** was barely visible.*
incite	*v* (to provoke) *It was the sight of so many police that **incited** the crowd to riot.* ➤ *n* **incitement**
incorporate	*v* (to include) *The sociology course **incorporated** courses in statistics and psychology.*
incredible	*adj* (hard to believe) *At first sight the results of the test seemed **incredible**.* ➤ *n* **incredibility**
indictment	*n* (*prep* **of**) (an accusation) *The low academic standards amounted to an **indictment** of the whole educational system.* ➤ *v* **indict**
indigenous	*adj* (native, belonging naturally to a place) *Such art forms are typical of the **indigenous** people in the region.*
induce	*v* (to lead or move by influence or persuasion) *It has been proved that music in supermarkets **induces** shoppers to buy more.* ➤ *n* **inducement**

indulge	*v* (to treat someone very generously) He **indulged** his daughter far too much, giving her almost everything she asked for. ➤ *n* **indulgence**
ineffectual	*adj* (having no effect) The manager was so **ineffectual** that the sales declined rather than rose. ➤ *n* **ineffectualness**
inert	*adj* (lacking independent power to move; not active) She gasped when she saw him lying **inert** on the floor.
infectious	*adj* (catching) It was only after several more children fell sick that they realized the disease was **infectious**. ➤ *n* **infection**; *v* **infect**
infested	*adj* (*prep* **with**) (inhabited in large numbers by something harmful) The whole area was **infested** with locusts. ➤ *n* **infestation**; *v* **infest**
infinitesimal	*adj* (tiny) It takes just an **infinitesimal** amount of the drug to cause hallucinations.
inflate	*v* (to make bigger) He found that the figures had been greatly **inflated** by including unsold stock.
influx	*n* (*prep* **of**) (an inflow) Following the discovery of gold there was a huge **influx** of people into the state.
infringe	*v* (to go against) The questioning of the suspect without a lawyer present **infringed** his civil rights. ➤ *n* **infringement**
infuse	*v* (*prep* **with, into**) (to fill with) The new trainer **infused** the whole team with enthusiasm and energy. ➤ *n* **infusion**
ingratiate	*v* (*prep* **with**) (to get into favor) He tried to **ingratiate** himself with her by buying her flowers.
ingredients	*n* (parts of a mixture) Unable to buy all the **ingredients**, she decided to cook a different dish.
inhabit	*v* (to live in a place) The Indians **inhabited** a small island just off the coast. ➤ *pn* **inhabitant**
inherit	*v* (*prep* **from**) (to receive as a result of the death of the previous owner) He **inherited** a fortune from his father. ➤ *n* **inheritance**
inhibit	*v* (*prep* **from**) (to repress) The presence of her father **inhibited** her from kissing her boyfriend. ➤ *n* **inhibition**; *adj* **inhibited**
initiate	*v* (to start; to begin) A party was given to **initiate** the new sales campaign. ➤ *n* **initiation**
innate	*adj* (quality present from birth) He had an **innate** ability to enthuse people.
innovation	*n* (a change; something new) IBM's new laptop computer has many unique **innovations**. ➤ *v* **innovate**; *adj* **innovative**

inquisitive	*adj* (asking many questions; curious) *The kitten was so **inquisitive** that it crawled up the chimney.* ➤ n **inquisition**; pn **inquisitor**
inscription	*n* (prep **in**) (writing in) *Someone had forgotten to write an **inscription** on the card.* ➤ v **inscribe**
insert	*v* (prep **in, into**) (to put inside) *She **inserted** a pacifier into the baby's mouth to stop it from crying.* ➤ n **insertion, insert**
insinuate	*v* (to suggest) *She made it sound like a joke but **insinuated** that he was mean with money.* ➤ n **insinuation**
inspire	*v* (to influence thought; create enthusiasm) *The book **inspired** him to try writing himself.* ➤ n **inspiration**
instance	*n* (an example) *She was so frightened of her landlord that in one **instance** she crossed the road rather than meet him in the street.*
instigate	*v* (to cause, to begin) *The discovery of yet another body **instigated** a search of the entire state.* ➤ n **instigation**; pn **instigator**
instill	*v* (prep **in, into**) (put ideas into mind) *Her parents had **instilled** in her a hunger for information.*
instrumental	*adj* (prep **in**) (means by which something is brought about) *That first concert was **instrumental** in making her decide to study music.*
insulate	*v* (to isolate) *To prevent anyone else getting an electric shock, he **insulated** the connection with tape.* ➤ n **insulation**
intact	*adj* (whole) *Much of the text was cut out but the main idea of the essay remained **intact**.*
integrate	*v* (prep **into**) (to coordinate; to unite) ***Integrating** barely developed countries into the EEC has proved difficult.* ➤ n **integration**
intensify	*v* (make stronger) *Her failure to return home **intensified** his worries.* ➤ adj **intense**
interact	*v* (to react mutually) *The two teams of scientists **interacted** positively once the research phase began.* ➤ n **interaction**; adj **interactive**
interim	*n* (the period between) *The course doesn't start for two weeks but in the **interim** I advise you to revise.*
intermittent	*adj* (coming and going at intervals) *From the woods came the **intermittent** call of an owl.*
interpret	*v* (to make out the meaning) *He **interpreted** the statistics to mean that the company was in trouble.* ➤ n **interpretation**

interrogate	v (to question) The police **interrogated** the thief for three hours but failed to learn where the money was hidden. ➤ n **interrogation**; pn **interrogator**
intersect	v (to cross) The two highways **intersect** close to the town of Boulder. ➤ n **intersection**
interstate	adj (between states) State laws prohibited **interstate** transport of dairy products.
intertwine	v (tie together) Increasingly, biology and engineering are becoming **intertwined**.
intransigence	n (non-flexibility) The meeting continued for hours but the **intransigence** of several directors prevented a successful conclusion.
intravenous	adj (entering into blood vessels) The doctors ordered the patient to be fed with an **intravenous** drip.
intrepid	adj (fearless) The head of the expedition had a reputation as an **intrepid** and experienced leader.
intricate	adj (complicated) The watch mechanism was so **intricate** that only an expert could fix it. ➤ n **intricacy**
intrude	v (prep **on**, **upon**, **in**) (to be in the way; to be an obstacle) The hotel manager apologized for **intruding** upon the guests. ➤ n **intrusion**; adj **intrusive**
intuitive	adj (instinctive) She discovered that she had an **intuitive** understanding of the subject. ➤ n **intuition**
invade	v (to make a hostile inroad) The German army **invaded** Russia without warning. ➤ n **invasion**
invalid	n (a sick person) He has been an **invalid** ever since the accident.
invaluable	adj (priceless) His help was **invaluable**, I couldn't have done it without him.
invariable	adj (always the same) His **invariable** hunger for information amazed her.
invert	v (to reverse position) He **inverted** the sauce bottle to get the last drop out. ➤ n **inversion**
invigorate	v (to provide energy) Every morning he **invigorates** himself with a swim.
invoke	v (to appeal to authority) The judge **invoked** an ancient law when ordering the arrest. ➤ n **invocation**
irrevocable	adj (unalterable) Their separation has become **irrevocable** so they've decided to divorce.

J

jab   *v* (to strike suddenly with a pointed instrument) *She **jabbed** him with her umbrella point and forced him to back away.*

jaded   *adj* (tired; uninterested from having had too much experience) *After years in the job he felt **jaded** and longed for a change.*

jagged   *adj* (rough, uneven) *She was unhurt by the fall but there was a **jagged** tear in her sleeve.*

jam   *v* (*prep* **into**) (to force into place that is too small) *More than twenty people **jammed** themselves into the office to study the exam results on display there.* ➤ n **jam**

jeopardize   *v* (to put at risk) *His cheating **jeopardized** the success of the entire team.* ➤ n **jeopardy**

jerk   *v* (to move suddenly) *She managed to **jerk** the gun out of his hand.* ➤ v **jerk**

juggle   *v* (to misrepresent, manipulate) *By **juggling** the figures, he managed to steal thousands of dollars.*

jut   *v* (*prep* **out**) (to stick out) *The sea-wall **juts** out far enough into the sea to create a small harbour.*

juvenile   *n* (youth) *Why don't you grow up instead of acting like a **juvenile**.* ➤ adj **juvenile**

juxtapose   *v* (*prep* **with**) (to place together) *The poor quality of the product, **juxtaposed** with the inadequate distribution system, persuaded the store to cancel their order.* ➤ n **juxtaposition**

K

keen   *adj* (eager)
Although not brilliant, she is a very **keen** student.

kin   *n* (family)
He listed a brother as his next of **kin** on the form.

kink   *n* (*prep* **in**) (sharp turn or twist) A **kink** in the rope caused the knot which prevented them from pulling the man to safety.

knack   *n* (*prep* **of**) (talent) Although he was polite, he had the **knack** of always saying the wrong things.

knit   *v* (*prep* **together**) (to join together) Because of her age, it took months for the bones fractured in the accident to **knit** together.

L

lag   *v* (to fail to keep up) At first he managed to keep up with the leaders of the race but then began to **lag** behind.

lament   *v* (to express sorrow) The entire nation **lamented** the death of the president. ➤ *n* **lament**

lanky   *adj* (tall and thin) He was so **lanky** that his brother nicknamed him 'Lamppost'.

laud   *v* (to praise) Following the success of the film, he was **lauded** by all the critics.

law-abiding   *adj* (obedient to the law) The governor of the state is known to be **law-abiding** and respectable. ➤ *pn* **law-abider**

lay   *adj* (non-professional) He prefers to be a **lay** preacher than to represent an organized religion. ➤ *pn* **layman**

league   *n* (*prep* **with**) (a group sided with) She's in **league** with them so anything you tell her will get back to them. ➤ *prep* **with**

legislation   *n* (laws) New **legislation** will be necessary to change the current trade imbalance. ➤ *v* **legislate**; *pn* **legislator**; *adj* **legislative**

legitimize   *v* (to make legal) You'll have to find a way to **legitimize** the business before the next tax audit. ➤ *n* **legitimacy**; *adj* **legitimate**

leniency   *n* (mild, tolerant) Because of his age, the judge showed **leniency** and only fined him. ➤ *adj* **lenient**

levy   *n* (*prep* **on**) (fines, taxes) The council raised the money by imposing **levies** on the ferry crossing.

libel   *v* (to defame in writing or pictures) The newspaper had to pay millions of dollars for **libeling** the author in their article on fraud. ➤ *n* **libel**; *adj* **libelous**

limb   *n* (a branch of something larger; arm, leg) He was lucky not to break one of his **limbs** in the crash.

limp	*v* (to function below capacity) *The company barely **limped** through last year but the future looks promising.* ➤ *n* **limp**
literate	*adj* (knowledgeable; well-read) *He's very **literate** and reads anything he can find.* ➤ *neg* **illiterate**
loaf	*v* (to be lazy and idle) *He **loafs** around all day and only opens a book when the boss appears.*
loathe	*v* (to hate; to detest) *Now she **loathes** him but she used to go out with him.* ➤ *adj* **loathsome**
lobby	*v* (to try to influence) *There are several arms companies **lobbying** to be given the laser beam contract.* ➤ *n* **lobby**; *pn* **lobbyist**
loot	*v* (to obtain valuables from the midst of destruction) *The town was **looted** by both armies as they passed through.* ➤ *n* **loot**; *pn* **looter**
loyal	*adj* (trustworthy) *He remained **loyal** to the company until a dispute over pay.* ➤ *neg* **disloyal**; *n* **loyalty**; *pn* **loyalist**
luminous	*adj* (giving out light) *Her father said nothing until she arrived home with her hair dyed **luminous** green.* ➤ *n* **luminosity**; *v* **illuminate**

M

maim   *v* (to injure for life) *Apart from the dead, hundreds were* **maimed** *as a result of the shelling.*

malign   *v* (to speak ill of, to speak falsely) *The actress felt she has been* **maligned** *by the director in his speech.* ➤ *adj* **malignant**

malpractice   *n* (failure of professional duty or standard) *A group of the disappointed investors are suing the accountancy company for* **malpractice**.

manipulate   *v* (to influence or cause indirectly) *Behind the scenes, he* **manipulated** *events to guarantee a favorable outcome.* ➤ *n* **manipulation**; *adj* **manipulative**

mansion   *n* (a large and imposing house; a residence) *The main home of the Kennedy family is a huge* **mansion** *overlooking the bay.*

marshal   *v* (to gather in good order) *The prime task of a lawyer is to* **marshal** *the facts so that they can be presented in a logical manner.* ➤ *pn* **marshal**

mature   *v* (to develop over time) *The idea needs to* **mature** *before it can be accepted.* ➤ *n* **maturity**; *adj* **mature**

meddle   *v* (*prep* **in**) (to interfere; to intrude) *The ambassador was formally asked not to* **meddle** *in the internal affairs of the country.* ➤ *adj* **meddlesome**

mediocre   *adj* (of poor quality) *The acting, direction and filming were excellent but the story was* **mediocre**. ➤ *n* **mediocrity**

menace   *v* (to threaten) *Despite all the money poured into law-enforcement, muggers continue to* **menace** *citizens.* ➤ *n* **menace**

mend   *v* (to repair) *The little girl asked him to* **mend** *the broken doll.*

mentor   *n* (teacher; mature guide) *My* **mentor** *at college was Professor Martins, who always helped me and gave me good advice.*

merger   n (a combination; joined businesses) *There are rumors of a **merger** involving several major airline companies.* ➤ v **merge** (prep **with**)

meteor   n (a small celestial body) *Most **meteors** burn up when they enter the Earth's atmosphere.* ➤ adj **meteoric**

meticulous   adj (to be careful about detail) *He took **meticulous** care composing the questions to ensure they only related to the course.*

mime   v (to act out without speaking) *Instead of answering, he held his jaw and **mimed** that he had a toothache.*

mingle   v (prep **with, among**) (to mix; to combine) *To avoid capture by the police, he **mingled** with the crowd.*

minuscule   adj (very small) *All that was visible was a **minuscule** trace of a red liquid that could have been blood.*

mitigate   v (to soften) *The only excuse he had to **mitigate** his disgraceful behavior was that he'd been drunk.* ➤ n **mitigation**

modulate   v (to vary the strength) *Not knowing which frequency to use, the scientists **modulated** the signal across a range of frequencies.* ➤ n **modulation**

molest   v (to annoy; to bother; to attack) *The sign warned women to jog only during daylight hours to avoid being **molested** by strange men.*

moron   n (a foolish person) *He may be the smartest student here but he still acts like a **moron**.* ➤ adj **moronic**

morsel   n (a small amount of food) *I'm starving and you haven't even left me a **morsel** of food.*

mortal   adj (not living eternally) *He may be the heavyweight champ but he's still **mortal** like us.* ➤ n **mortality**

multifaceted   adj (varied) *The task we have been set is **multifaceted**, so many skills will be called upon.*

multiply   v (to grow in number) *Overnight the crowds **multiplied** until the whole square was full.* ➤ n **multiplication**

munch   v (to chew noisily) *So many people were **munching** popcorn, I couldn't follow the movie.*

mutate   v (to change form) *It was about a scientist who **mutated** into a complete monster.* ➤ n **mutation**; adj **mutant**

mutual   adj (having the same feelings; shared) *Apart from a **mutual** love of music, they have nothing in common.*

muzzle   v (to keep quiet) *The press were **muzzled** about the matter with threats of legal action.*

myriad   n (prep **of**) (a great number) *The sky was clear and **myriads** of stars were visible.*

N

nadir   *n* (the lowest point) *The situation on the stock market reached its **nadir** on Monday with the greatest fall in stock prices in years.*

necessitate   *v* (to require) *The situation is so critical that it **necessitates** a complete change of policy.* ➤ *adj* **necessary**

negate   *v* (to make invalid) *Your overall marks are high enough to **negate** the need to resit the exam but they are still below average.* ➤ *n* **negation**

neglect   *v* (to ignore; to give insufficient attention) *It was clear from his ragged and dirty clothes that he had begun to **neglect** himself.* ➤ *n* **neglect**; *adj* **negligent**

negotiate   *v* (to try to agree) *The senators **negotiated** all through the night and it wasn't until morning that they reached an agreement.* ➤ *n* **negotiation**; *pn* **negotiator**

nocturnal   *adj* (living by night) *As a jazz musician, he lived a **nocturnal** existence, sleeping all day and working all night.*

numb   *adj* (without sensation) *The temperature sank below zero and his feet were **numb** with cold.*

nurture   *v* (to feed; sustain) *Throughout his years of imprisonment, he **nurtured** a deep hatred for the police.*

O

oasis	*n* (a place with water in the desert; or a positive exception) *With such familiar music playing, the bar was like an **oasis** in the unfriendly city.*
obey	*v* (to follow an order) *He was such a well trained officer that he **obeyed** his commander without thinking.* ➤ *n* **obedience**; *adj* **obedient**; *neg* **disobey**
oblige	*v* (to do someone a favor) *When she complained about the noise, he **obliged** her by turning down the music.*
obliterate	*v* (to get rid of all traces) *Before leaving, Bond **obliterated** all traces of his presence in the room.*
oblivion	*n* (the condition of being completely forgotten) *Slowly the memories of that terrible night sank into **oblivion** and her life returned to normality.*
oblivious	*adj* (*prep* **to**) (forgetful; unaware) *The racing driver seemed **oblivious** to the danger right up to the fatal crash.*
obscure	*adj* (not easily seen or understood) *For normal people, the book was too **obscure** to read but the critics loved it.* ➤ *n* **obscurity**; *v* **obscure**
obsequious	*adj* (over-obedient; servile) *His **obsequious** manner whenever the boss was present annoyed his colleagues.*
obsolete	*adj* (no longer useful; outdated) *New computer systems have made old methods of data processing **obsolete**.* ➤ *n* **obsolescence**
obstinate	*adj* (stubborn; unyielding) *Even as a child he was **obstinate** and couldn't be persuaded to do anything against his will.* ➤ *n* **obstinacy**
obstruct	*v* (to get in the way; to block) *The angry strikers used their trucks to **obstruct** the gate to the factory.* ➤ *n* **obstruction**; *adj* **obstructive**
occupation	*n* (job; profession) *His original **occupation** was teaching but now he's a famous rock star.* ➤ *adj* **occupational**
offspring	*n* (children) *The female bear with her **offspring** was seen ambling down the road.*

offend	v (to cause annoyance) Her selfish attitude **offended** everyone in the class. ➤ adj **offensive**; pn **offender**
ominous	adj (threatening) The latest outbreak of fighting looks **ominous** for the peace accord. ➤ n **omen**
omit	v (to leave out) When he was questioned, he foolishly **omitted** telling the police about the accident. ➤ n **omission**
opponent	pn (competitor) His **opponent** in the election was a third year economics student. ➤ v **oppose**; adj **opposite**
opportunistic	adj (taking advantage of favorable situations with no thought of the consequences) He had a reputation for being **opportunistic** and using every chance to his advantage. ➤ n **opportunity**
optimize	v (to do the best possible) She **optimized** her chances for passing the exam by carefully researching previous papers. ➤ n **optimum**
oration	n (a formal speech) The professor continued talking for hours until everyone was bored with his **oration**. ➤ pn **orator**
orchard	n (a group of fruit trees) As a child he used to steal apples from the **orchard** behind his house.
ordeal	n (a difficult or painful experience) The hostages managed to stay cheerful throughout their lengthy **ordeal**.
orient	v (to choose a direction) He's a good student but needs to **orient** himself and settle on a goal in life. ➤ n **orientation**
ornate	adj (highly decorated) Even the palace gate was **ornate**; decorated with a massive coat of arms.
orthodox	adj (conventional) I advise you to complete the course in **orthodox** medicine before exploring alternative therapies. ➤ n **orthodoxy**
outlaw	v (to make illegal) Several states have **outlawed** the sale of scanners to prevent phone frauds. ➤ pn **outlaw**
output	n (production; yield) In order to increase **output** a night shift will be hired at the factory.
outrageous	adj (very offensive or shocking) The general's **outrageous** remark offended all his guests.
overall	adj (general; comprehensive) We shall have to wait for the end of the year to get an **overall** picture.
overstate	v (to exaggerate) The builder deliberately **overstated** the extent of the damage so he could charge more money for the repairs. ➤ n **overstatement**
overwhelming	adj (very powerful; not allowing argument) There is an **overwhelming** case for increasing our investment.

P

pact   *n* (a treaty; an agreement) *The peace **pact** signed in Ohio appears to be working.*

palatable   *adj* (tasty; savory) *He found the local food rich but **palatable**.* ➤ *neg* **unpalatable**

pamphlet   *n* (a single leaf brochure) *The **pamphlet** clearly stated that no attempt should be made to open up the machine.*

pander   *v* (*prep* **to**) (to satisfy unpleasant wishes) *He may enjoy alcohol but I see no reason why I should **pander** to him and provide whiskey.*

parable   *n* (a short tale illustrating morality or religion) *Religious teachers often use **parables** to make difficult ideas easy to understand.*

paramount   *adj* (most important) *More guards have been recruited because the need for increased security is **paramount**.*

paranormal   *adj* (impossible to explain scientifically; supernatural) *Everyday several hundred incidents involving the **paranormal** are reported to the FBI.*

participant   *pn* (*prep* **in**) (someone who takes part) *All three **participants** in the quiz show were teachers.* ➤ *n* **participation**; *v* **participate**

passion   *n* (*prep* **for**) (intense emotion, liking) *He had a **passion** for hot spicy food.* ➤ *adj* **passionate, impassioned**

patent   *n* (legal rights to an invention) *His family grew rich having inherited the **patent** to the machine.* ➤ *v* **patent**

pauper   *n* (a very poor person) *The failure of the bank and the closure of the factory left him a **pauper**.*

pedigree   *n* (registered ancestry) *The dog had certificates proving its **pedigree** for ten generations.* ➤ *adj* **pedigree**

peek   *v* (to take a brief look) *The burglar **peeked** through the window to see if anybody was home.*

penalize	v (to punish) The company was **penalized** with a fine for not finishing the project within the contracted time. ➤ n **penalty**
penetrate	v (to pass through; to enter) The Pentagon is investigating how the aircraft managed to **penetrate** American air defenses. ➤ n **penetration**
pensive	adj (thoughtful) The old man sat staring out of the window with a **pensive** expression.
perforated	adj (having lines of small holes in something) Please tear the paper along the **perforated** line. ➤ n **perforation**
perilous	adj (full of danger) Despite his wounds, he still managed to complete the **perilous** journey over the mountains. ➤ n **peril**; v **imperil**
periphery	n (area that surrounds) High walls and rolls of barbed wire characterize the **periphery** of the jail. ➤ adj **peripheral**
permanent	adj (long lasting, constant) The museum is a **permanent** reminder of the horrific events that took place. ➤ n **permanence**
permeate	v (prep **into**, **through**) (to pass into) The cold was so intense that it **permeated** the walls of the house.
permissible	adj (allowed) It is not **permissible** to smoke in any public place. ➤ n **permission**; v **permit**
perpetual	adj (continuing forever; constant) During spring there is a **perpetual** threat of avalanches. ➤ n **perpetuity**
perspective	n (viewpoint) Seen from a long term **perspective**, the situation is quite promising.
persuade	v (to convince) He tried his best to **persuade** her to come home with him but she refused. ➤ n **persuasion**; adj **persuasive**
pertinent	adj (relevant) I am afraid that such facts are not **pertinent** to this discussion. ➤ n **pertinence**
pessimist	pn (one who always takes a gloomy view) He's such a **pessimist** that he carries an umbrella even when the sun is shining. ➤ n **pessimism**; adj **pessimistic**
petition	n (a formal request) More than a thousand people signed the **petition** that was handed to the governor. ➤ v **petition**
phlegmatic	adj (slow, calm) Most journalists tend to be rather **phlegmatic** and rarely get excited about anything.
pierce	v (to make a hole) He had his ear **pierced** for an earring last week.

pilfer	*v* (to steal small amounts or things of little value) *They say the reason he was fired was because he was caught **pilfering** photocopier paper.*
pillar	*n* (a column; a responsible person who upholds traditional values) *Until his arrest everybody considered him to be a **pillar** of society.*
pinch	*v* (to press hard between one's fingers) *The secretary screamed when she felt someone **pinch** her in the elevator.*
pinpoint	*v* (to identify exactly) *We've got a rough idea but we still haven't been able to **pinpoint** the cause of the breakdown.*
pioneer	*v* (to be the first) *Edison is now recognized for **pioneering** research into the practical applications of electricity.* ➤ *pn* **pioneer**
pirate	*v* (to steal and develop a concept) *Under the latest agreement the Chinese will stop **pirating** CD-ROM computer programs.*
pity	*n* (compassion) *Once she had loved him but now she only felt **pity**.* ➤ *v* **pity**; *adj* **pitiful**
placate	*v* (to appease, console) *She was so upset by the news that he was unable to **placate** her.*
plateau	*n* (a broad plain) *The new shopping mall will be constructed on a large **plateau** overlooking the beach.*
plausible	*adj* (believable but doubtful) *The idea sounded **plausible** but hardly convincing.* ➤ *n* **plausibility**
plea	*n* (an appeal) *The bank manager refused even to listen to her **pleas** for more time to pay back the loan.* ➤ *v* **plead**
plethora	*n* (an amount greater than is needed) *The manager was confronted with a **plethora** of complaints from angry customers.*
plump	*adj* (a full and round shape) *Despite all her efforts to diet, she remained rather **plump**.*
pollute	*v* (to contaminate; to make dirty) *The chemical company insisted that the new plant would not **pollute** the river.* ➤ *n* **pollution**; *adj* **pollutant**
ponder	*v* (*prep* **over**) (to consider carefully) *He **pondered** over the matter for several days before announcing his decision.* ➤ *adj* **ponderous**
portray	*v* (to describe, depict) *The actor **portrayed** the general as a weak and indecisive character.* ➤ *n* **portrayal**
posterity	*n* (future generations) *The concept behind the memorial was to create something to be handed down to **posterity**.*

postpone	*v* (to delay) *The match was **postponed** because of the storm.* ➤ n **postponement**
postulate	*v* (to put forward as fact; accept as true) *The scientist had **postulated** that it was possible and was surprised when the experiments failed.*
practitioner	*n* (someone with a skill) *As a **practitioner** of law, he knew the legal system had its faults.*
prank	*n* (a trick; a joke) *It had only been a college **prank** but unfortunately they had taken it seriously.* ➤ pn **prankster**
preach	*v* (to seriously lecture) *He was an old fashioned teacher who **preached** discipline and hard work.* ➤ pn **preacher**
precaution	*n* (prep **against**) (action taken to avoid a future accident or problem) *As a **precaution** against devaluation of local currencies, he keeps his money in dollars.* ➤ adj **precautionary**
precede	*v* (to go before) *An introduction will **precede** the main performance.* ➤ n **precedent**
precept	*n* (a rule; a command) ***Precepts** such as the ten commandments governed his life.*
precisely	*adv* (exactly) *The time is ten o'clock **precisely**.* ➤ n **precision**
precocious	*adj* (prematurely adult) *She was so **precocious** that even as a ten-year-old she wore make-up.*
precursor	*n* (an early sign) *Pentium chips are now regarded as merely **precursors** of far faster chips.*
predator	*n* (a hunter) *The deer has to be wary of wolves and other **predators**.* ➤ adj **predatory**
predict	*v* (to tell what will happen in the future; to foretell) *The company has **predicted** even greater profits in the coming year.* ➤ n **prediction**; adj **predictable**
predilection	*n* (prep **for**) (a preference) *The director's **predilection** for fast cars is well known.*
predispose	*v* (prep **to, toward**) (to make susceptible) *I should suggest saving money but I'm rather **predisposed** to the idea of borrowing more and investing.* ➤ n **predisposition**
predominate	*v* (to have the main influence; to be greater in number) *Becoming a victim of crime **predominates** as the principle fear of the aged.* ➤ n **predominance**; adj **predominant**
prejudice	*n* (prep **against**) (a bias) *Following his conviction, he harbored a deep **prejudice** against the Federal Tax Department.* ➤ adj **prejudicial**
prelude	*n* (a preliminary event preceding a more important one) *This period of calm was a **prelude** to weeks of intense activity.*

premonition	n (a feeling that something is going to happen) Despite the assurances of the doctors, he had a **premonition** that he was going to die.
preserve	v (to keep in original form) The old painting had been well **preserved** and the colors had kept their brilliance. ➤ n **preservation**
prestigious	adj (admired; highly valued) He has joined an extremely **prestigious** company so he should do well. ➤ n **prestige**
pretension	n (a false claim to possess skill or expertise) Although he was the company director, he had no **pretensions** that he could do everything himself.
prevail	v (to continue in fashion; to succeed) Some of the traditional customs still **prevail** among those living in isolated areas. ➤ n **prevalence**; adj **prevalent**
prevaricate	v (to resist telling the truth) At first the suspect **prevaricated** but eventually he confessed to the crime. ➤ n **prevarication**
prey	v (prep **on**) (to hunt; to commit violence or robbery) Gangs of youths from the ghetto **prey** on the occupants of cars passing through. ➤ n **prey**
priceless	adj (too valuable to price) Donated to the museum by an oil tycoon, the portrait was a **priceless** example of the artist's work.
primary	adj (most important; first) The **primary** objective was to halt further spending.
primeval	adj (ancient; from the beginning of time) The plain had once been covered by a **primeval** forest.
primitive	adj (basic) When the electricity was cut they depended on a **primitive** pump for water.
prior	adv (prep **to**) (before in time or importance) **Prior** to the meeting, the managing director studied the file carefully. ➤ n **priority**
privilege	n (special advantage) The president's job allows many **privileges** but also involves many sacrifices.
probe	v (to conduct a thorough examination) The committee **probed** into every aspect of the case before reaching a decision. ➤ n **probe**
procrastinate	v (to delay or postpone action) Instead of **procrastinating**, why don't you get started on the job? ➤ n **procrastination**
proffer	v (to offer politely) He **proffered** the stranger a cigar.

profound	*adj* (deep) A ***profound*** *silence followed the gun-shot.*
prohibition	*n* (*prep* **on**) (a ban; era of the banning of alcohol in the US) *Many made fortunes from selling alcohol during* ***Prohibition***. ➤ *v* **prohibit**
proliferate	*v* (to increase rapidly) *Isolated at first, in the 80s the number of AIDS cases suddenly* ***proliferated***. ➤ *n* **proliferation**
prolific	*adj* (productive) *Freud was a* ***prolific*** *writer and published no less than eighty-two papers on his findings.*
promote	*v* (to publicize) *The new soap powder will be* ***promoted*** *all over the country using TV and newspaper advertising.* ➤ *n* **promotion**
prompt	*v* (to cause or urge) *The disaster* ***prompted*** *the government to revise the safety regulations.*
promulgate	*v* (to make known; to declare officially) *It is believed the new law will be* ***promulgated*** *next month.*
prop	*v* (*prep* **up**) (to support) *The government has decided to buy up huge amounts of dollars to* ***prop*** *up its value.* ➤ *n* **prop**
prophesy	*n* (a forecast) *The manager gave a* ***prophesy*** *that his team would win the title.* ➤ *v* **prophesy**; *pn* **prophet**
proponent	*pn* (supporter) *One of the bill's* ***proponents*** *argued that such a law was vital for the economy.*
propose	*v* (to suggest) *The president* ***proposed*** *a two percent cut in the interest rate.* ➤ *n* **proposition**
proprietor	*n* (one who owns a business) *The shop* ***proprietor*** *kept a loaded shotgun beneath the counter.* ➤ *adj* **proprietary**
proscribe	*v* (to forbid, ban) *To avoid a general uprising, the government* ***proscribed*** *the protest meeting.*
prosecute	*v* (to bring before a court) *In the future, all those found carrying a knife will be* ***prosecuted***. ➤ *n* **prosecution**
prosper	*v* (to succeed; to thrive) *Their business began to* ***prosper*** *when they moved to their new location.* ➤ *n* **prosperity**; *adj* **prosperous**
protrude	*v* (to push outward; to project) *When he saw the nail* ***protruding*** *from the tyre, he understood what had caused the accident.* ➤ *n* **protrusion**
provoke	*v* (*prep* **into**) (to cause; to incite) *He was released on the grounds that he had been* ***provoked*** *into assaulting the drunk.* ➤ *n* **provocation**; *adj* **provocative**
proximity	*n* (nearness) *He was relieved to discover that there was a hospital in the* ***proximity***.

prudent   *adj* (careful; wise) *The Continental Congress made the **prudent** decision to continue trading with English importers.* ➤ *n* **prudence**

purchase   *v* (to buy) *They decided to **purchase** the Boeing because of its ability to fly longer distances without refueling.* ➤ *n* **purchase**

purify   *v* (to cleanse) *The explorers had to **purify** the water by boiling it.* ➤ *n* **purification, purity**

pursue   *v* (to chase after; to follow a course of action) *He **pursued** a career as a lawyer before standing for election.* ➤ *n* **pursuit** (*prep* **of**)

Q

quagmire   *n* (a negative situation that is difficult to escape from) The project became bogged down in a **quagmire** of trivial objections.

quake   *v* (to tremble violently) The first indication of the earthquake was when the pots and pans began to **quake** on the shelf.

quandary   *n* (*prep* **about, over**) (a feeling of not knowing what to do) Unable to pay the debt, she found herself in a **quandary** over whether to sell her car or TV.

quarry   *n* (a pursued animal or person) When the detective saw the blood stains, he realised his **quarry** had been injured.

quash   *v* (to reject something already decided upon) The appeal court **quashed** the sentence given him by a lower court because the evidence was considered unsafe.

quell   *v* (to make quiet; to subdue) The police used water cannons to **quell** the disturbance.

quench   *v* (to satisfy thirst) The driver admitted that he had **quenched** his thirst with beer and not a soft drink as he had earlier claimed.

query   *v* (to question) Many **queried** the findings of the committee but they were unable to change them.

quest   *n* (a search) More money has been spent on the **quest** for a cure for cancer than any other disease.

quirk   *n* (a strange habit) She was known to have many **quirks** such as her refusal to use the telephone. ➤ *adj* **quirky**; *adv* **quirkily**

quintessential   *adj* (typical) Wearing that old school tie and bowler hat, he looks like a **quintessential** Englishman.

R

ramble   *v* (to wander idly; to talk or write without purpose) *The lecturer **rambled** on for an hour and several students fell asleep.*

rancor   *n* (spiteful hatred) *Hopefully the inhabitants of the city will forget their **rancor** and learn to live in peace.*

random   *adj* (chance) *The workers hired were chosen at **random** to prevent any ill feeling.*

rash   *adj* (with little care) *It is now clear that the decision to buy the Tornado was **rash** and unwise.*

ratify   *v* (to approve; to confirm officially) *The law will have to be **ratified** before it can be applied.* ➤ *n* **ratification**

rationalize   *v* (to find a reasonable explanation) *He bet his last money on the horse having **rationalized** that it wasn't enough to buy a meal.* ➤ *n* **rationality**; *adj* **rational**

raw   *adj* (unrefined, undeveloped) *The player had a **raw** ability that needed developing.*

raze   *v* (to destroy completely down to the ground) *The fire **razed** fifteen houses before it was brought under control.*

reassure   *v* (to comfort) *The news of the oil discovery helped to **reassure** the shareholders that profits would rise.* ➤ *n* **reassurance**

rebut   *v* (to contradict; to push away) *Senator Lewis was chosen to **rebut** the proposal.* ➤ *n* **rebuttal**

recall   *v* (to remember) *She was able to **recall** some important details about the man.* ➤ *n* **recollection**

recede   *v* (draw back) *Now that the rain has stopped, the danger of flooding has **receded**.* ➤ *n* **recession**

recipient   *pn* (*prep* **of**) (someone who has received) *The **recipient** of this year's prize will be announced next week.* ➤ *v* **receive**

reciprocate   *v* (to do something in return) *The senate decided to **reciprocate** the enemy's peace initiative by lifting the embargo against them.* ➤ *n* **reciprocation**

recite	*v* (to repeat from memory) *The lawyer **recited** all the facts of the case.* ➤ n **recitation**
reckless	*adj* (not cautious; not careful) *His license was suspended for two years for **reckless** driving.*
recluse	*n* (a person who chooses to live apart from society) *After his wife died he became a **recluse**; refusing to see anyone but his closest friends.* ➤ adj **reclusive**
reconcile	*v* (to adjust to something negative) *The downturn in the economy meant she had to **reconcile** herself to lower wages.* ➤ n **reconciliation**
recourse	*n* (a source of help) *Following the failure of the business, his only **recourse** was to sell his car.*
recurring	*adj* (repeating) *The **recurring** theme of the film was that crime doesn't pay.* ➤ n **recurrence**
redeem	*v* (to recover) *His fans were disappointed by his performance in the first set but he **redeemed** himself by winning the second.* ➤ n **redemption**
refined	*adj* (noble; attractive) *By her **refined** manners, it was clear she was well educated.* ➤ n **refinement**; v **refine**
refurbish	*v* (to make new again) *It would take too much money to **refurbish** such a broken down house.* ➤ n **refurbishment**
refute	*v* (to prove something is incorrect) *The dean **refuted** the argument that standards were falling by pointing out the exam successes that had been achieved.*
regress	*v* (to lapse, to deteriorate) *He seemed to be recovering but then his condition **regressed**.* ➤ n **regression**; adj **regressive**
rehearse	*v* (to practice, particularly acting) *He **rehearsed** the speech for days until it was perfect.* ➤ n **rehearsal**
reiterate	*v* (to say again; to repeat) *Let me **reiterate** the main points of the matter.*
relapse	*n* (the return of a condition) *The patient suffered a **relapse** and returned to the hospital.* ➤ v **relapse**
relent	*v* (to soften in attitude) *At first he refused to give her more money but eventually **relented**.*
reliable	*adj* (dependable) *He's a **reliable** man and I have no hesitation in giving this reference.* ➤ n **reliability**; v **rely** (prep **on**)
relinquish	*v* (to give up possession) *When the vote went against him, the chairman was forced to **relinquish** his position.*
reluctant	*adj* (unwilling, hesitant) *She was **reluctant** to accept the invitation because she knew he would ask her to go home with him.* n **reluctance**

reminisce	*v* (to remember nostalgically) *Having dinner, they **reminisced** about their days as students.*
remnant	*n* (something left over) *A **remnant** of cloth was found hooked on the barbed wire.*
remonstrate	*v (prep **with**, **about**)* (to express disapproval or opposition) *I **remonstrated** with him about the journey because I thought it was dangerous.*
renowned	*adj* (famous) *The author, **renowned** for his book on royalty, will be appearing next week.*
repel	*v* (to drive back) *The army **repelled** the enemy's first attack but then they were made to retreat.* ➤ *adj* **repellent**
reproach	*v (prep **for**)* (to blame; to disapprove) *The police officer merely **reproached** him for speeding.* ➤ *n* **reproach**
repulse	*v* (to drive back; to repel) *She was **repulsed** by his arrogance.* ➤ *adj* **repulsive**
resemble	*v* (to have a similar appearance, to be like) *He resembles his father in more ways than one.* ➤ *n* **resemblance**
reside	*v* (to live in a certain place) *She works in Manhattan but **resides** out of town.* ➤ *n* **residence**; *pn* **resident**
residue	*n (prep **of**)* (traces left) *All he found was the **residue** of a liquid in the glass.*
resilience	*n* (endurance) *Her **resilience** helped her to survive the ordeal.* ➤ *adj* **resilient** *(prep **to**)*
resolute	*adj* (firm; determined) *Despite opposition from his colleagues, he remained **resolute** in his decision.* ➤ *n* **resolution**
respond	*v (prep **to**)* (to answer; to react) *If he fails to **respond** to the treatment further tests will be necessary.* ➤ *n* **response**; *adj* **responsive**
restrain	*v* (to control; to limit) *The animal was so strong that they couldn't **restrain** it.* ➤ *n* **restraint**
retain	*v* (to keep in one's possession; to hold) *Although most of his possessions were seized, he was allowed to **retain** his house.* ➤ *n* **retention**
retard	*v* (to delay; to hold back) *The drug doesn't cure the disease but is able to **retard** its progress.*
reticent	*adj* (unwilling to speak) *The banker was **reticent** when asked about the missing money.* ➤ *n* **reticence**
retort	*v* (to give a quick or sharp reply) *The congressman **retorted** angrily that he knew nothing about the matter.* ➤ *n* **retort**
retract	*v* (to take back) *After being threatened with a libel action, the newspaper **retracted** the article about her.* ➤ *n* **retraction**

revelation   n (something revealed, disclosure) *The newspaper published the **revelation** that he had been an army deserter.*

revenue   n (money; income) *The state gets most of its **revenue** from taxes.*

reverse   v (to go in the opposite direction) *The Supreme Court can **reverse** the decision of any lower court.* ➤ n **reversal** (*prep* **of**)

revive   v (to return to consciousness or to life) *The unconscious boxer was **revived** with smelling salts.* ➤ n **revival**

revoke   v (to cancel) *Because of the incident his permit to carry a gun was **revoked**.*

rigorous   adj (energetic) *Before the practice match the team has to complete an hour of **rigorous** exercise.*

rinse   v (to wash in clean water) *She made him **rinse** the soap off the plates.*

rivalry   n (contest, competition) *The **rivalry** for the position was intense.* ➤ *pn* **rival**; *adj* **rival**

roam   v (to wander) *He had to put up a fence to keep his horses from **roaming** into another field.*

role   n (a character played by an actor; a function) *Her main **role** in the company was to prepare presentations.*

rotate   v (to turn in a circle) *The officers were **rotated** among different camps to stop them forming friendships with the prisoners.* ➤ n **rotation**

roughly   adv (approximately) *The budget of the company is **roughly** equal to that of some third world countries.*

rural   adj (of the country) *He moved out of the city to settle in a small **rural** community.*

rusty   adj (oxidized) *The lock was too **rusty** to open.* ➤ n **rust**

S

sag — *v* (to bend downwards, to droop) *The wind was so strong that the middle of the bridge began to **sag**.*

sagacity — *n* (good judgment; wisdom) *The governor is widely respected for his **sagacity**.* ➤ *adj* **sagacious**

sanctuary — *n* (private or protected place) *When life was too hectic, he retired to the **sanctuary** of his office.*

sanction — *n* (penalty) *The UN voted to impose **sanctions** after the government executed its political prisoners.*

savage — *adj* (primitive and cruel) *Normally he was passive but turned **savage** after drinking alcohol.*

scant — *adj* (meager, little) *The report gave **scant** attention to the sales figures, concentrating more on productivity.*

scarce — *adj* (insufficient quantity) *During the war luxury goods were **scarce**.* ➤ *n* **scarcity** (*prep* **of**)

scatter — *v* (to throw or move in all directions) *The demonstrators **scattered** when the police charged.*

schism — *n* (separation caused by difference of opinion) *A wide **schism** grew between the official Communist party and the reformists.* ➤ *adj* **schismatic**

scoff — *v* (*prep* **at**) (to speak derisively) *The new manager openly **scoffed** at the teachings of his predecessor.*

scoop — *v* (to dip into with a spoon or a cupped hand) *He **scooped** out a spoonful of jam and swallowed it.*

scope — *n* (*prep* **of**) (the range or extent of something) *The questions were beyond the **scope** of his knowledge.*

scornful — *adj* (disdainful; aloof) *Once elected, he became **scornful** of the advice of his assistants.* ➤ *n* **scorn**; *v* **to scorn**

scrape — *v* (to wear off; to cut off in pieces) *His mother told him to **scrape** the mud off his shoes before entering the house.*

scrub — *v* (to wash vigorously by rubbing) *She was unable to **scrub** the stain off the jacket.*

scrutiny	n (close and careful examination) *The report was the subject of close **scrutiny** as soon as it was published.* ➤ v **scrutinize**
seal	v (to close) *He forgot to **seal** the letter before posting it.*
secure	v (to make safe) *The commander ordered the fence to be **secured** by nightfall.* ➤ n **security**; adj **secure**; neg **insecure**
segment	n (a division; a part of something) *The city was divided into three **segments**.*
segregate	v (prep **from**) (to set apart) *In the United States, black Americans used to be segregated from white Americans.* ➤ n **segregation**; neg **desegregate**
seize	v (to take; to claim ownership) *The authorities **seized** his property to pay his debts.* ➤ n **seizure**
sensitize	v (to make receptive) *The paper had to be specially **sensitized** before use.* ➤ n **sensitivity**; adj **sensitive**
sentry	n (a guard, a soldier) *Despite an increase in the number of **sentries** outside the White House, yet another attempt was made to shoot the president.*
sequester	v (to stay in isolation) *The jury were kept **sequestered** in a hotel until they reached a verdict.*
sever	v (to cut into two parts) *He managed to **sever** the rope with his penknife.* ➤ n **severance**
shabby	adj (worn-out; faded) *Despite his wealth, he always wore **shabby** clothes.*
shame	v (to cause embarrassment) *He **shamed** her before her friends by being drunk when he came around.* ➤ n **shame**; adj **shameful**
shatter	v (to break into many pieces) *The injuries caused by the accident **shattered** her dreams of becoming an athlete.*
shawl	n (a covering for a woman's head and shoulders) *She was given a **shawl** to put on before entering the mosque.*
shed	v (to let fall off) *A snake **sheds** its skin regularly.*
shift	v (to change position or direction) *When his opponent wasn't looking the chess player **shifted** one of his pieces.*
shrewd	adj (able in practical affairs; clever, quick-minded) *Although she had no formal education, she proved a **shrewd** businesswoman.*
shrink	v (to decrease in size) *Because of the drought, the population of the region has **shrunk** considerably.*

shrug	*v* (to raise the shoulders in a gesture of doubt or indifference) *Instead of answering, he merely **shrugged**.* ➤ *n* **shrug**
shutter	*n* (a cover to keep out light or rain) *The **shutter** in the lens of the camera was faulty.*
sieve	*n* (a sorting utensil) *He used a **sieve** to wash away the mud and find the grains of gold.*
sift	*v* (*prep* **through**) (to make a thorough investigation) *It took the detectives several weeks to **sift** through all the reports.*
simulate	*v* (to imitate; to copy) *The engine was tested under conditions of extreme heat to **simulate** tropical conditions.* ➤ *n* **simulation**
simultaneously	*adv* (at the same time) *They reached the door **simultaneously** and bumped into each other.*
single-handedly	*adv* (to do something alone) *Joshua Slocum was the first man to sail **single-handedly** around the world.*
sinuous	*adj* (winding; curving) *From the spacecraft, the Great Wall of China could be seen as a **sinuous** thread.*
sip	*v* (to drink a little at a time) *He **sipped** the beer slowly to make it last longer.* ➤ *n* **sip**
skeptical	*adj* (*prep* **of**) (not easily convinced; doubting) *Despite all her attempts to convince him, he remained **skeptical** of her intentions.* ➤ *n* **skepticism**; *pn* **skeptic**
skim	*v* (*prep* **through**) (to read quickly and superficially) *He **skimmed** through the papers on the train.*
slant	*v* (to give a bias) *Instead of remaining objective, the article was **slanted** in support of the candidate.*
slap	*v* (to hit with an open hand) *He **slapped** the hysterical woman.* ➤ *n* **slap**
slaughter	*v* (to kill, often in large numbers) *The cattle seemed to sense they were about to be **slaughtered**.* ➤ *n* **slaughter** (*prep* **of**); *pn* **slaughterer**
slave	*n* (unpaid servant) *The Romans depended on **slaves** to build and maintain their empire.* ➤ *v* **enslave**; *adj* **slave**
slay	*v* (to kill) *They found the gun used by the killer to **slay** his victims.* ➤ *pn* **slayer**
sleazy	*adj* (cheap; disreputable) *Having run out of money, he stayed in a **sleazy** hotel.* ➤ *n* **sleaze**
sleet	*n* (a mixture of snow and rain) *When the temperature dropped the rain turned to **sleet** and snow.*
slit	*v* (to cut) *He **slit** the throat of the sheep with a sharp knife.* ➤ *n* **slit**

sluggish	adj (not easily aroused; slow to respond) The pills made him feel **sluggish** which was the underlying cause of the accident.
slum	adj (impoverished, run-down) Having won the lottery, he moved from an inner city **slum** area to the suburbs. ➤ n **slum**
slump	n (economic failure) The worst **slump** in American history began in the 1920s.
smolder	v (to burn with little smoke and no flame) The fire was still **smoldering** days after being extinguished.
snatch	v (to grab abruptly or hastily) He was finally arrested after he tried to **snatch** an old woman's bag.
sneak	v (to move quietly and secretly) He tried to **sneak** out of the house when no one was looking.
soar	v (to fly high) The eagle **soared** high above the trees hunting for prey.
sober	adj (not drunk) The blood test proved he hadn't drunk any alcohol and was completely **sober**. ➤ n **sobriety**
soil	v (to dirty; contaminate) The room looked clean but the bed sheets had been **soiled** with what looked like ink.
solar	adj (from the sun) **Solar** energy has replaced conventional forms of energy as a heating source throughout the state.
solemn	adj (grave, serious) The judge's expression was **solemn** as he pronounced the sentence. ➤ n **solemnity**
soothe	v (to calm) The doctor gave the hysterical woman some pills to **soothe** her. ➤ v **soothe**
sophisticated	adj (refined; worldly) It was clear from her smart clothes and restrained manner that she was an extremely **sophisticated** woman. ➤ n **sophistication**
span	v (to extend from one side to another) The world's longest suspension bridge is being built in Japan and will **span** the four-mile distance between two islands. ➤ n **span**
spasm	n (sudden tightening of muscles) Malaria can cause violent **spasms** but is rarely life threatening. ➤ adj **spasmodic**
species	n (a group with a common appearance) Radiation from nuclear testing has contaminated vast areas of the Pacific and is thought to have caused the mutation of a **species** of crab.
specific	adj (detailed; precise; exact) The **specific** cause of the accident is uncertain but sabotage is suspected. ➤ n **specification**
speck	n (a very small spot or fragment of something) He cleaned the room so well there wasn't a **speck** of dirt visible.

spectator	n (one who watches) Despite the fact there were only fifteen **spectators** in the audience on the first night, the show was a success.
speculate	v (prep **on**, **about**) (to guess; to think about something) As yet, scientists can only **speculate** on the true nature of the universe. ➤ n **speculation**
spill	v (prep **out**, **over**) (to spread beyond limits) The area has become so overcrowded that people are beginning to **spill** out of residential zones and settle up in the hills.
spiral	v (to rise continuously) The costs of the project have **spiraled** out of control.
sporadic	adj (happening from time to time) The minister's speech was interrupted by **sporadic** applause.
sprawl	v (prep **out**) (to stretch out) She came home to find a man **sprawled** out on the sofa, fast asleep.
squash	v (to crush) The company hired a team of strong men to **squash** more passengers into the train carriages.
squat	v (to crouch down) Before the celebrations, the Indians **squatted** down to discuss the events.
stabilize	v (to become firm and steady) At first the doctors feared for his life but then his condition began to **stabilize**. ➤ n **stability**; adj **stable**
stack	v (to put several things on top of each other) The check-out girl **stacked** the heaviest items in the bottom of the bag, placing the eggs on top. ➤ n **stack**
stagger	v (to walk unevenly) He managed to **stagger** home from the bar without help despite being extremely drunk.
stale	adj (not fresh; old) The bread was so **stale** it was inedible.
static	adj (not moving) This is a bad time for us, sales are almost **static**.
steadfastly	adv (to stick firmly) The company **steadfastly** keeps to its schedule but delays still occur.
stellar	adj (of the stars) This Apollo flight will conduct a series of **stellar** mappings.
sterilize	v (to get rid of microbes) It was discovered that the dentist had failed to **sterilize** the equipment. ➤ n **sterilization**; adj **sterile**
stimulate	v (to start or to increase activity) The government reduced taxes to **stimulate** the economy. ➤ n **stimulus, stimulation**
straddle	v (to be positioned equally on either side of something) The village **straddles** a low hill.

strain	*n* (tension; stress) *Not knowing if he would live or die was a source of much **strain**.* ➤ *v* **to strain**
stranded	*adj* (unable to continue) *He missed the last bus home and was **stranded** in the village until the next day.*
stringent	*adj* (strict) *To stop petty thefts, the company introduced **stringent** regulations.*
strive	*v* (to make great efforts; to struggle) *You must **strive** to get here on time.*
stunt	*v* (to retard normal growth) *The doctors discovered his growth was being **stunted** by a hormone deficiency.*
subsequent	*adj* (following) *Such questions will be handled in **subsequent** lectures.*
substantiate	*v* (to prove) *Even though he felt he was right, he was unable to **substantiate** his theories.*
substantive	*adj* (of independent existence; not subsidiary) *There were **substantive** reasons for the decline of the empire.*
substitute	*v* (**prep for, with**) (to use something in place of another; to replace) *The trainer decided to **substitute** his star player with an untried junior.* ➤ *n* **substitute, substitution**
subtract	*v* (to take away from something) *Costs and overheads have to be **subtracted** to work out profits.* ➤ *n* **subtraction**
succinct	*adj* (brief; summarized) *Fortunately, the introductory speech was **succinct** and entertaining.*
sue	*v* (to bring to court) *When they refused to refund him the money, he had to **sue** them.*
sultry	*adj* (hot and moist weather) *She hated the **sultry** jungle climate.*
supersede	*v* (to replace) *A new model will be introduced next year to **supersede** the current model in production.*
surfeit	*n* (an excessive amount) *There was a **surfeit** of food at the party, so much of it was not eaten.*
surly	*adj* (rude; arrogant) *Despite his **surly** manner, she grew to like him.* ➤ *n* **surliness**
surmise	*v* (to guess) *With no trace of him to be found, the police could only **surmise** that something had happened to him.*
surpass	*v* (to outdo; to go beyond) *The latest sales figures show the company has **surpassed** its own estimates.*
surplus	*n* (extra to needs) *He was pleased to announce that a **surplus** of funds existed.*
survey	*n* (**prep of, into**) (inquiry into something) *According to a government **survey**, unemployment has risen by fifteen per cent.* ➤ *v* **survey**

survive *v* (to outlive; to manage to stay alive) *By eating roots and leaves, he managed to **survive** until the rescue party found him.* ➤ n **survival** (*prep* **of**)

sustain *v* (to endure; to keep going) *To **sustain** him until his broken jaw healed, the doctors prescribed a diet of vitamin enriched fluids.* ➤ n **sustenance**

swamp *v* (to overwhelm by excess) *Following the publication of his book, he was **swamped** by congratulatory messages.*

swarm *n* (a large number of moving insects) *It is believed that the unusual weather caused the bees to **swarm**.* ➤ n **swarm**

swerve *v* (to turn aside; to veer) *The accident occurred after the driver **swerved** to avoid another vehicle.*

swift *adj* (rapid) *The reaction of the police to the phone call was extremely **swift**.*

T

taciturn   *adj* (not wanting to speak; silent) *Although his injuries healed, he remained psychologically scarred and became very **taciturn** and withdrawn.*

tack   *v* (to fasten loosely; to add on) *An amendment had been **tacked** to the conclusion of the report.*

tact   *n* (diplomacy) *Despite his academic success, he had no **tact** and was always saying the wrong things.* ➤ *adj* **tactful**; *neg* **tactless**

taint   *v* (to contaminate) *She was convinced the report was **tainted** by the inclusion of opinions rather than facts.*

tally   *n* (an account; a score) *The final **tally** showed an increase of more than fifteen per cent.* ➤ *v* **tally**

tamper   *v* (to interfere in a harmful manner; to meddle) *It was clear someone had **tampered** with the controls because their positions had changed.*

tangle   *v* (*prep* **with, in**) (to mix in a confused manner) *The closure of the main road caused the city traffic to become **tangled** with commuter traffic.* ➤ *n* **tangle**

tapered   *adj* (smaller at one end) *The end of the knife is **tapered** to a fine point.*

tarnish   *v* (to discolor; to spoil) *The scandal **tarnished** his reputation and put an end to his hopes of becoming a political candidate.*

temperate   *adj* (moderate) *Fortunately the region has a **temperate** climate and rarely experiences either intense heat or cold.*

temporarily   *adv* (for only a short time) *The sign said the telephone was **temporarily** out of order.*

tentative   *adj* (uncertain; possible) *They decided to fix a **tentative** date for the next meeting.*

tepid   *adj* (slightly warm) *That day the temperature of the sea was quite **tepid** and certainly warm for winter.*

terminate	*v* (to bring to an end) *Because of his prolonged absences, his contract was **terminated**.* ➤ n **termination**
testify	*v* (to give evidence before a court) *Two witnesses **testified** that he had been present at the scene of the murder.* ➤ n **testimony**
texture	*n* (quality of surface) *The **texture** of the material was quite rough to touch.*
theorize	*v* (to put forward an idea) *He **theorized** that extra energy was due to static electricity.* ➤ n **theory**; adj **theoretical**
therapy	*n* (treatment) *The doctors ordered that the patient should be given a course of the new **therapy**.* ➤ adj **therapeutic**
thread	*v* (to put through a small hole) *Her eyesight was so poor that she was unable to **thread** a needle.* ➤ n **thread**
thrifty	*adj* (economically careful) *After his wages were reduced, he became more **thrifty**.* ➤ n **thrift**
throng	*n* (a crowd) *Outside the court, a great **throng** of well-wishers were gathered to congratulate him on his release.*
tiptoe	*v* (to walk stealthily and quietly) *The burglar **tiptoed** across the hall to avoid waking the occupants of the house.*
tilted	*adj* (not straight, uneven) *One leg of the table was slightly short so the table **tilted** to one side.*
toil	*v* (to work hard) *He **toiled** away in the mines until his health suffered.* ➤ n **toil**
token	*adj* (symbolic) *Prevented by Congress from sending an aircraft carrier to the war zone, the President sent only a **token** force of a hundred men.* ➤ n **token** (prep **of**)
tolerant	*adj* (prep **of**) (having a fair attitude toward opposing views) *She liked him because he was **tolerant** of other people's opinions.* ➤ n **tolerance**; neg **intolerant**
topple	*v* (to overturn) *The army took over and **toppled** the president from power.*
torture	*v* (to inflict extreme pain on someone) *His wife accused him of mental **torture** because he made her go on a diet.*
touchy	*adj* (sensitive; irritable) *Abortion remains a **touchy** subject in many southern states.*
toxic	*adj* (poisonous) *The company was convicted of releasing **toxic** chemicals into the sea.* ➤ n **toxin**
trace	*v* (to locate) *The detective managed to **trace** the woman by checking through her tax records.* ➤ n **trace** (prep **of**)
tract	*n* (a short piece of writing, often religious or political) *The **tract** was published in a magazine.*

tranquil

tranquil   *adj* (peaceful; quiet) The **tranquil** atmosphere in the cove was disrupted by the arrival of a powerful motorboat. ➤ *n* **tranquillity**

transact   *v* (to conduct; perform or carry out business) The sale of the land was **transacted** as soon as the new law came into force. ➤ *n* **transaction**

transcend   *v* (to rise above; to surpass) The guitarist was so good, his music **transcended** anything Dave had ever heard before. ➤ *adj* **transcendent**

transform   *v* (*prep* **into**) (to change in appearance) The building of a shopping mall **transformed** the area from a quiet backwater into a noisy commercial center. ➤ *n* **transformation**

transfusion   *n* (injection) When the money for the project ran out, the banks provided a **transfusion** of funds. ➤ *v* **transfuse** (*prep* **into, of**)

transition   *n* (*prep* **from, to**) (a period of change) The **transition** from being a mere assistant to becoming a director was a difficult phase.

transmit   *v* (to send, impart) He tried to **transmit** the message on another frequency but there was still no response. ➤ *n* **transmission**

transparent   *adj* (allowing light to pass through) The material was so thin, it was almost **transparent**. ➤ *n* **transparency**

traverse   *v* (to move across) The railroad had to **traverse** a deep gorge. ➤ *n* **traverse**

treacherous   *adj* (not to be trusted; dangerous) The road up the side of the mountain was winding and **treacherous**. ➤ *n* **treachery**

trend   *n* (a course; a tendency) The **trend** of people moving to the suburbs continues on the west coast. ➤ *adj* **trendy**

tributary   *n* (a river that flows into a larger one) The Ohio River is a **tributary** of the Mississippi River.

trigger   *v* (to set off a reaction) The increasing demand for apartments in the city **triggered** a big price rise. ➤ *n* **trigger**

trivial   *adj* (of little importance) In general your test was very good; you only made a few **trivial** mistakes.

troupe   *n* (a group of actors) The **troupe** will present six different plays during the season.

tug   *v* (to pull something with effort) A small boat **tugged** the ship into the harbor.

tumble   *v* (to fall in a rolling manner) She tripped and **tumbled** down the stairs.

tumult   *n* (noisy commotion) *He could not be heard over the **tumult** of angry voices.*

tutor   *v* (to teach) *Tim wants someone to **tutor** him before the test.*
➤ *pn* **tutor**

U

ultimate   *adj* (final) Her **ultimate** goal is to receive her degree and return to her country of origin.

unanimous   *adj* (in full accord; by common consent) The vote to lift the sanctions was **unanimous**. ➤ n **unanimity**

uncouth   *adj* (rude) The **uncouth** manners of the author shocked everyone at the reception.

undercut   *v* (to sell cheaper than a competitor) By buying cheap and selling cheap, supermarkets are able to **undercut** smaller rivals.

undergo   *v* (to experience) He **underwent** a serious operation but now he's comfortable.

undermine   *v* (to weaken) Her discovery greatly **undermines** current theories.

unite   *v* (to join together) **United**, the two companies would become a major force in the business. ➤ n **unity**

universal   *adj* (present or occurring everywhere) Support for the proposal has been **universal**.

uphold   *v* (to support) The decision has been **upheld** by the court and has to be obeyed.

urban   *adj* (town) Society has become more **urban** over the last decade.

usher   *v* **(prep in)** (to lead in) The turn of the century is **ushering** in a period of global uncertainty.

utilitarian   *adj* (many uses; practical) It's a **utilitarian** device that can perform a wide variety of functions.

V

vacant — *adj* (empty) The house has been **vacant** for two years. ➤ *n* **vacancy**

vagrant — *n* (one who moves from place to place without a fixed abode) The clothes of the **vagrant** were torn and dirty.

vanish — *v* (to disappear) The child was astonished when the magician caused the coin to **vanish**.

vanity — *n* (foolish pride) Her **vanity** led her to lie about her age. ➤ *adj* **vain**

variation — *n* (*prep* **of**) (a different form of something; a change) The music was a **variation** of an old folk song. ➤ *v* **vary**; *adj* **varied**

variety — *n* (a collection of many different things or types) The jacket came in a **variety** of styles.

vehemence — *n* (forcefulness; intensity) She spoke with such **vehemence** that he was frightened. ➤ *adj* **vehement**

veil — *v* (to hide)
The sun was **veiled** by thick fog. ➤ *n* **veil**

vendor — *n* (one who sells something) He bought a pack of cigarettes from a street **vendor**.

venomous — *adj* (poisonous) The snake was known to be extremely **venomous**. ➤ *n* **venom**

verify — *v* (to make certain of the truth; to confirm) He decided to telephone the manager to **verify** the information. ➤ *n* **verification**

versatile — *adj* (having varied uses; flexible) Plastic is a very **versatile** material and has many applications. ➤ *n* **versatility**

vestige — *n* (a small remaining sign; a trace) Having heard the boy's explanation, a **vestige** of doubt remained.

vet — *v* (to check background and eligibility) Before he was invited to join the company he was thoroughly **vetted**.

viable — *adj* (able to succeed) Doing the work himself was the only **viable** alternative. ➤ *n* **viability**

vibrate	*v* (to move back and forth rapidly) *The car **vibrates** at high speed.* ➤ *n* **vibration**; *adj* **vibrant**
vicarious	*adj* (to experience something through another person) *Although he couldn't drive himself anymore, being a passenger in her car gave him a **vicarious** thrill.* ➤ *n* **vicariousness**
vice	*n* (a moral failure) *It was the love of alcohol, his worst **vice**, that finally killed him.*
vicinity	*n* (**prep of**) (nearness) *There was only one shop in the **vicinity** of the school.*
vigilance	*n* (watchfulness) *Thanks to the **vigilance** of the police, the thief was caught.* ➤ *adj* **vigilant**
vindicate	*v* (to prove correct in the face of opposition or disbelief) *The experiment has to a great extent **vindicated** Einstein and proved he was on the right track.* ➤ *n* **vindication**
vindictive	*adj* (spiteful) *In her old age, she became **vindictive** toward him and often accused him of a variety of sins.*
virtue	*n* (moral goodness; a good characteristic) *Perhaps the best **virtue** of the car is its acceleration.* ➤ *adj* **virtuous**
vis-à-vis	*prep* (with regard to) *What's your opinion **vis-a-vis** the new law?*
vocalize	*v* (to make audible) *After weeks of silence, she decided to **vocalize** her thoughts.* ➤ *adj* **vocal**
volunteer	*v* (to offer to do something) *To help the charity, he **volunteered** his services.* ➤ *n* **volunteer**; *adj* **voluntary**
vulnerable	*adj* (**prep to**) (weak) *The young are especially **vulnerable** to drugs.* ➤ *n* **vulnerability**

W

wade   *v* (to walk through shallow water) *He **waded** into the waves up to his knees.*

wane   *v* (decrease in size or intensity) *They decided to wait until the moon had **waned**.*

warily   *adv* (cautiously) *Frightened by the noise, she opened the door **warily**.*

warrant   *v* (to justify) *The crowd may have been unruly but it certainly didn't **warrant** such an extreme police assault.* ➤ *n* **warrant**

wax   *v* (grow larger) *Due to the lack of light, they waited for the moon to **wax**.*

wayward   *adj* (non conforming; irregular) *He sat watching the **wayward** flight of the eagle.*

wealthy   *adj* (rich, prosperous) *She grew **wealthy** by buying and selling property.* ➤ *n* **wealth**

weed   *v* (*prep* **out**) (to extract something bad) *The manager wanted to **weed** out the trouble-makers from the staff.*

whim   *n* (a sudden fancy or wish) *She decided to go to Paris on a **whim**.*

wholesale   *adj* (sold in large quantities) *The **wholesale** price of the items was much cheaper than the shop price.*

wile   *n* (a trick) *He used every **wile** he could think of to persuade her.* ➤ *adj* **wily**

wither   *v* (to lose freshness; to dry up; to fade) *By the time she was forty, her beauty had begun to **wither**.*

withhold   *v* (*prep* **from**) (to keep back) *Despite hours of questioning, the thief **withheld** the information from the police.*

wrath   *n* (great anger) *Fearful of his **wrath**, she remained silent.* ➤ *adj* **wrathful**

wrinkle   *v* (to crease) *The shirt was too **wrinkled** to wear and had to be ironed.* ➤ *n* **wrinkle**

Y

yelp *v* (to cry out sharply; usually in reference to dogs) *The dog **yelped** when the stone hit it.*

yield *v* (to give) *Despite months of research, the experiments failed to **yield** the answer.*

Z

zealot *n* (an enthusiastic person; a fanatic) *The president was assassinated by a religious **zealot**.*

B

Structure and Vocabulary Checks

Structure

Part I

Choose the phrase which best completes each sentence.

1. The recipient ———— was kept for five years under house arrest.

    (a) for the Peace Prize
    (b) to the Peace Prize
    (c) of the Peace Prize
    (d) in the Peace Prize

2. ————, he found a rare letter written by Washington.

    (a) To sift through
    (b) Sifting in
    (c) Sifting by
    (d) Sifting through

3. It is now believed that the attack on the ferry ————

    (a) is ushering in the first war.
    (b) ushered to the first war.
    (c) ushered by the first war.
    (d) ushered in the first war.

4. Although I can appreciate the logic of the plan, I fail to see its ————

    (a) pertinencation to the current situation.
    (b) pertinence to the current situation.
    (b) pertinment to the current situation.
    (b) pertening to the current situation.

Structure

5 The terrible weather, _____ the oncoming darkness, made the journey impossible.

   (a) juxtaposition with
   (b) juxtaposed to
   (c) juxtaposed with
   (d) in juxtaposing with

6 He came under considerable pressure from the committee yet refused to _____.

   (a) be pandered to their wishes.
   (b) pander for their wishes.
   (c) be pandering to their wishes.
   (d) pander to their wishes.

7 He took daily walks and worked out in a gym three times a week but his predilection _____ led to his contracting a rare blood disease.

   (a) to fatty foods
   (b) against fatty foods
   (c) for fatty foods
   (d) by fatty foods

8 The professor _____ before dismissing the class.

   (a) expounded with the theory
   (b) had expounded by the theory
   (c) expounded on the theory
   (d) expounded theory

9 Touring the refugee camp, the team of doctors were shocked by the _____

   (a) deprivement they saw.
   (b) deprivation they saw.
   (c) depriving they saw.
   (d) depriveness they saw.

10 The engine and mechanical parts are clearly in good condition but there are spots of rust that detract _____

   (a) from its value.
   (b) its value.
   (c) to its value.
   (d) up its value.

Structure

Part 2

Find the word or phrase which is wrong in each of these sentences.

11 Needless to say, following the incident the public's
        A   B
    aversion of guns has grown to become an important
        C   D
    political issue.

12 Although the pilot managed to eject safely in the
                       A   B
    doomed aircraft, this latest crash has been a severe blow
                            C   D
    to the company.

13 Although emaciated and thin, the two climbers still
                     A
    managed to joke with the crew of the rescue helicopter.
       B   C   D

14 What made the fight even more exciting was that it
        A   B
    was known that the champion nursed a grudge for his
       C   D
    opponent.

15 His heartless arrogance contrasted completely with her
        A   B
    haughtiness so her friends were amazed when the
        C   D
    engagement was announced.

16 The daring acrobat seemed totally oblivious with the
                         A   B
    danger and won a standing ovation from the audience.
             C   D

Structure

17. Knowing Stalin to be obstinate, as well as stubborn,
          A   B
    the commander of the camp merely nodded
                      C
    his agreement.
      D

18. The encountement shocked her and thereafter she
         A   B
    made a point of always carrying a gun when she visited
          C
    the surrounding villages.
         D

19. The money was certainly instrumental with making
        A   B
    her choose to accept the job but she was also excited
    by the prospect of doing research again.
        C   D

20. The latest figures issued by the Federal Reserve suggest
                  A   B
    that the current recede is most likely a short-term
                C   D
    situation.

Vocabulary

Find the word or phrase which most closely matches the underlined section in each sentence.

1. In many respects the natures of the chimpanzee and man are <u>alike</u>.
   - (a) akin
   - (b) copied
   - (c) identical
   - (d) duplicated

2. The company announced that the <u>ceremonial opening</u> of the new store would take place at the end of the month.
   - (a) indictment
   - (b) multiplication
   - (c) reciprocation
   - (d) inauguration

3. If I were you, I'd think twice before <u>agreeing</u> to his suggestion.
   - (a) equivocating
   - (b) compelling
   - (c) asserting
   - (d) acceding

4. The latest report <u>proves incorrect</u> the suggestion that the business is unprofitable.
   - (a) relinquishes
   - (b) testifies
   - (c) undercuts
   - (d) refutes

5. By the time the storm had <u>died down</u> it was almost morning.
   - (a) abated
   - (b) hinged
   - (c) relinquished
   - (d) scattered

Vocabulary

6 Although exports had increased, the total annual <u>income</u> was down by fifteen percent.

(a) revenue
(b) purchase
(c) omission
(d) deterioration

7 Bond was the only man there who could <u>open</u> the computer file without supervision.

(a) reject
(b) reiterate
(c) survey
(d) access

8 The <u>total</u> effect of erosion over so many years has placed the structure in danger.

(a) accumulative
(b) remarkable
(c) erroneous
(d) dilapidated

9 Her exam results were poor but that didn't <u>discourage</u> her from applying for a scholarship.

(a) detract
(b) jeopardize
(c) deter
(d) portray

10 It took hours of persuasion before he <u>agreed</u> to the request.

(a) donated
(b) acquiesced
(c) submitted
(d) demanded

11 At first she had great difficulty working the cement mixer but eventually she grew <u>used to</u> it.

(a) adapted to
(b) to like
(c) accustomed to
(d) fond of

Vocabulary

12. The electric drill came complete with a number of <u>parts</u> to do a variety of jobs.

    (a) insinuations
    (b) particulars
    (c) accessories
    (d) invocations

13. The signing of the peace treaty was <u>praised</u> by all the delegates present.

    (a) rewarded
    (b) condoned
    (c) arraigned
    (d) acclaimed

14. The next morning her father <u>lectured</u> her for an hour on the evils of drink.

    (a) preached to
    (b) preceded
    (c) sequestered
    (d) transcended

15. The new chemical had been <u>taken</u> from a complex synthetic material.

    (a) abstracted
    (b) retained
    (c) digested
    (d) transferred

16. The police found a large amount of money that the suspect was unable to <u>explain</u>.

    (a) recount
    (b) account for
    (c) replicate
    (d) deny

17. The thief and his <u>partner</u> were arrested still in possession of the stolen painting.

    (a) practitioner
    (b) parasite
    (c) activator
    (d) accomplice

Vocabulary

18 The police chased after the bank robber but lost track of him in the subway.

(a) lagged behind
(b) pursued
(c) hindered
(d) heeded

19 The jury were convinced the police had interfered with the evidence and acquitted the thief.

(a) contrived
(b) tarnished
(c) tampered with
(d) predisposed

20 Even though he knew the man was guilty, he had very little information to support the belief.

(a) scant
(b) unreliable
(c) frightening
(d) censored

21 The jury found him guilty but fortunately the judge showed him compassion.

(a) law-abiding
(b) leniency
(c) levies
(d) gratitude

22 Their profits are up fifteen percent but that will be reversed as soon as the tax penalties come into effect.

(a) sanctions
(b) interpretations
(c) schism
(d) legitimacy

23 Meticulous care was taken to check the findings yet errors were still made.

(a) adequate
(b) multifaceted
(c) little
(d) detailed

Vocabulary

24 The prosecution tried to ameliorate the skepticism of the jury by calling the police chief to the witness box.

(a) increase
(b) libel
(c) legalize
(d) lessen

25 The samples were analyzed and found to contain an infinitesimal amount of the drug.

(a) infinite
(b) substantial
(c) tiny
(d) immeasurable

26 The court decided that the team had impinged upon the player's rights by failing to tell him about the transfer.

(a) cured
(b) relapsed
(c) vindicated
(d) harmed

27 Much as he hated the assignment, he had no choice except to reconcile himself to the new circumstances.

(a) adjust
(b) refute
(c) inhabit
(d) endeavor

28 His equivocal manner in answering questions concerning his speech was disappointing.

(a) medium
(b) enticing
(c) authentic
(d) evasive

29 At a later meeting he reiterated the belief that an anti-AIDS drug would be found.

(a) denied
(b) confirmed
(c) repeated
(d) rejected

Vocabulary

30 Throughout his career as a lawyer he <u>nurtured</u> the dream of becoming a politician.

(a) sustained
(b) ignored
(c) suppressed
(d) hid

Answers

Structure

Part 1

1. C
2. D
3. D
4. B
5. C
6. D
7. C
8. C
9. B
10. A

Part 2

11. C (aversion to)
12. B (from the)
13. A (thin is the same as emaciated)
14. D (grudge against)
15. C (haughtiness is the same as arrogance)
16. B (oblivious to)
17. B (stubborn is the same as obstinate)
18. A (encounter)
19. B (instrumental in)
20. C (recession)

Answers

Vocabulary

1. A
2. D
3. D
4. D
5. A
6. A
7. D
8. A
9. C
10. B
11. C
12. C
13. D
14. A
15. A
16. B
17. D
18. B
19. C
20. A
21. B
22. A
23. D
24. D
25. C
26. D
27. A
28. D
29. C
30. A